"*Star Child: A Mother's Journey Through Grief* by Jennifer Martin is a beautifully crafted tribute to a young son's life and death, which lands in the heart gently, like a feather from an angel's wing."
—Maria Housden, author, *Hannah's Gift: Lessons from a Life Fully Lived*

"Jennifer Martin's son, Kelly, was a remarkable spirit of love and grace wrapped for twenty-three years in a body that was inexorably weakening. But her gifted account of his life and death brings insights that take the reader to new and perhaps untouched places of discovery and empathy. *Star Child* reveals a depth of sorrow and a victory of transcendence that makes the grief of 'goodbye' reach into your heart and soul, both stirring pain and delivering peace. This is a stellar new entry into the world of hope and healing."
—Andrea Gambill, editor
Grief Digest magazine

"Jennifer is a transparent soul and her reflections heal us all."
—Karen Carpenter Calhoun, hospital chaplain

Star Child

Star Child

~

A Mother's Journey Through Grief

Jennifer J. Martin

iUniverse, Inc.

New York Lincoln Shanghai

Star Child
A Mother's Journey Through Grief

Copyright © 2006 by Jennifer J. Martin

iUniverse books may be ordered through booksellers or by contacting:

iUniverse
2021 Pine Lake Road, Suite 100
Lincoln, NE 68512
www.iuniverse.com
1-800-Authors (1-800-288-4677)

ISBN-13: 978-0-595-40216-8 (pbk)
ISBN-13: 978-0-595-84592-7 (ebk)
ISBN-10: 0-595-40216-X (pbk)
ISBN-10: 0-595-84592-4 (ebk)

Printed in the United States of America

Sometimes we are privileged to live with great souls. Their time with us is *always* too brief—yet ever so tender. But in their absence, they leave behind enough stardust for us to find our way to our center and back—wherein lies the path to our hearts, our souls and our healing.

To my beloved son, friend and teacher, Kelly Wayne Hales
August 26, 1967–February 5, 1991

To my beloved unborn baby daughter, Sarah, whose hand I never got to hold, but who will forever embrace my heart.

To the following children, parents and families who continue to be a part of my healing journey...

Clarissa Victoria Alderete
April 29, 1976–August 18, 1977
Daughter of Joe V. Jr. and Chris D. Alderete
*

Stephen James Atencio
November 8, 1946–March 8, 1991
Son of Agapito P. and Elouise Atencio
*

Michael Benishek
October 24, 1969–January 22, 1994
Son of Linda Svoboda
*

Brance Rueben Bergeron
July 24, 1978–July 24, 1978
Son of Charles and Julie Bergeron

*

Kelly James Carmody
November 16, 1978–December 1, 1987
Son of Mitchell and Barbara Carmody
Brother of Meagan Carmody
*

Christopher Dale Chavez
July 19, 1964–August 4, 1985
Son of Gary R. and JoAnn Chavez
*

Damien Zachary Cord
October 3, 1968–Yesterday
Son of Alex Cord
*

Michael George del Rio
March 15, 1966–November 29, 1997
Son of Carlos and Collette del Rio
Brother of Carlos M., Roxanne and Denise
*

Jeremy John Fumia
November 12, 1972–November 19, 1972
Son of Chuck and Molly Fumia
*

Jenny Garcia-Hayden
December 27, 1985–January 26, 2004
Daughter of Humberto Garcia Piedra and Ann Hayden
*

Diana Monica Garza
September 29, 1967–January 6, 1968
Daughter of Ricardo J. Garza Sr. and Diana J. Doria

*

Shanti Giovanna
February 25, 1977
Unborn daughter of Rashani
*

Douglas S. Goeble
October 30, 1964–April 20, 1991
Son of Bud and Sherry Goeble
*

Judy Gambill Grossman
November 13, 1958–January 12, 1976
Daughter of the late Jim and Andrea Gambill
Sister of Scott Gambill
Wife of TJ Grossman
Mother of Tom Grossman III
*

Charlie Guevara
February 17, 1972–August 6, 1991
Son of Christina M. Guevara
*

Douglas Wade Hall
December 13, 1960–June 11, 1978
Son of Don and Joan Hall
*

Charles Christopher Harris
September 11, 1945–February 16, 1965
Son of Christina Harris

*

Cyndee Kite
October 23, 1955–May 7, 1993
Daughter of the late Bill and Ginny Kite
*

Norma Jean Lara
December 28, 1975–February 14, 1993
Daughter of Mary Lara Mena
*

Jennifer Nell Lawrence
December 3, 1968–October 27, 1979
Daughter of Judith Manerud Lawrence
*

Heath A. Lewis
September 25, 1986–April 14, 1991
Son of Nancy A. Lewis
*

Stephen Crawford Lindsay
January 15, 1963–August 11, 1979
Son of James Irwin and Rose Marie Johnson Lindsay
Brother of five siblings
*

Richard Littlefield
November 7, 1969–May 22, 1991
Son of Guy and the late Joyce Littlefield
*

Michael Anthony Long
March 13, 1964–January 12, 1991
Son of Phyllis Long
Brother of Michelle Long Held

*

Kathleen Compian Lopez
August 7, 1968–April 4, 1993
Daughter of Tony Lopez and Carmen Compian
Sister of Anthony Compian
*

Hannah Catherine Martell
September 9, 1990–August 3, 1994
Daughter of Maria Housden
*

Preston Blake Mewhinney III
July 14, 1965–December 3, 1990
(Killed by a drunk driver)
Son of Sandee Mewhinney Johns
*

Michael Mowrey
February 8, 1985–August 31, 1992
Son of Jane and Gary Mowrey
*

Martha "Marti" Allison Nichols
August 1, 1967–October 21, 1989
Daughter of Diane G. Robertson
*

Lee Rabalais
March 26, 1982–May 20, 1996
Son of Donnie and Brenda Rabalais
Brother of Courtney Rabalais

*

Christopher Scott Rice
June 10, 1968–July 18, 1990
Son of Clarence Stewart and Carolyn Harris Rice
*

Ruben Roque Jr.
September 7, 1977–July 20, 1993
Son of Ruben G. Roque
*

Carlos Raul Sánchez
June 25, 1978–October 29, 1999
Son of Dennis and Loraine Sánchez
*

Jeffery Scott Tollefson
April 12, 1959–July 21, 1992

John Allen Tollefson
November 15, 1960–July 24, 2002
Sons of Gaylord and Marilyn Tollefson
*

Spencer Trainer
March 30, 1977–August 31, 1993
Son of Gil and Diana Trainer
*

Scott Anthony Villarreal
December 21, 1976–September 24, 1993
Son of Homer and Sandra Villarreal
Brother of Sean A. Villarreal

*

Victoria Lee Walston
September 1, 1967–May 6, 1974
Daughter of Gary and Dona Walston
*

Jason Gresham Wofford
March 26, 1980–October 24, 1990
Son of John and Marianne Wofford
*

Ty Young
May 23, 1974–December 7, 1991
Son of Sue Stiles

The deep emptiness of saying goodbye
becomes the doorway of awakening.

—*Rashani*

Contents

Star Child

"Come with me," the angel said, "Return to the stars." And the child leaned into the angel's arms, her diamond blue-white wings enfolded him and covered him with stardust to warm him for the journey home.

No cracking sounds of thunder or the shrill cries of a seagull mark this passage—only the still sound of your sweet soul leaving, as silent as your voice and beating heart. Fly now through the canyons, past the sun and the moon, remembering the way you came before. Slip freely and softly through the ancient doorway into the realm of eternity.

Take with you all the love you can carry, but leave enough for me to feel your presence; for I will need that love to find my way through the darkness. For the light that was your soul has left me.

Years from now, I will find you again and together we will soar away from this place—this place that kept me separate from you. And I will leave behind my body, the pain and the tears, taking with me all the joy and spiritual wisdom I finally found amidst the vast brokenness of your death.

Written June 1997, on the beach in Port Aransas, Texas

Acknowledgments

My sincere thanks go out to the poets and authors whose writing and poetry appear within these pages and so immeasurably enriched this work. Your words are etched in my soul.

With a grateful heart, I offer a special dedication to honor the following people who have played such important roles in both Kelly's life and mine, as well as being an intimate presence in my healing journey:

Joan Upton Hall, my wonderful editor, for your assistance and encouragement;

My writing critique group members: Bob Hill, Brendan Moore, and Gary Walston. Thank you for your belief in my writing and for the immense gift of your friendship;

Dona Walston for opening up your home to the critique group and for your delicious cooking which nurtured us all;

Joysa Maben Winter, my goddaughter, whose contributions and editing have enriched this writing beyond the horizon of love. (Many of the quotes that open chapters are ones she found throughout the years and lovingly forwarded to me.) She gifted me with her amazing talent and abilities as a journalist and transformed the manuscript into its final polished form. You're the best, Yehudit Simcha;

Buddy Bradshaw, LPC, LMFT, for being Kelly's and my friend, for your wisdom, laughter, healing soul and for showing our family about real love;

The late Michael L. Flynn, MD, and his family. Dr. Flynn's wisdom and skill gave me six more years with my son;

Felix "Dr. G" Gonzales, MSHP, FD/Emb, for being Kelly's hero, mentor and especially his friend who encouraged and believed in him;

and Ricardo A. Riojas, MD, for your heart and healing.

To the following special friends:

Peg Armstrong for teaching me about how to live after loss and for your enduring belief in me;

Lyn Belisle, for your love of art and Kelly;

Dortha Beers, for your beautiful love and friendship;

Cecelia Britton, for the vastness of our friendship and for the sweet memory of your healing hands on Kelly;

Mike Britton, for being a sensitive, joyful man and teaching Kelly how to be one;

Karen Carpenter Calhoun, for your abounding compassion, prayers of renewal and guidance of the Forever Loved group;

George Camarillo and his family—for allowing Kelly to be part of your family, for loving him and sharing the warmth of your friendship and the joy of shared laughter;

The late Mike del Rio, for being Kelly's best friend, my *other son,* for that special time we danced together and for the delight that you were in my life, and to Mike's parents, Carlos and Colette, for loving Kelly;

Joysa Gilbreath, for your abiding friendship, love, and tender care of me when Kelly died;

Phyllis Long, for your love, the shared journey of loss and your belief in my writing—from the beginning;

Dean Kirkpatrick, for being my friend and Kelly's and for flying for us all;

The Georgia and Dennis Nisi family, for love and acceptance of Kelly and for the cannoli he so loved;

Peggy Olson, for our soul/friend connection, for your love along the way, for your smile and your heart;

Randy Reines, for being a devoted friend to Kelly, for the chess games and the treasured photographs of Kelly;

Kani Sagebird, for your gentle care and love and for that special Easter Sunday at Kelly's grave;

Jeanette Schneider, for being there *always,* for being my forever caring soul-friend and for loving me and Kelly;

Ron Thornson, Reggie (Fresh) and Shirley, for road trips, for friendship, love and laughter and for "Lucky";

Beth Nisi Troilo, for your beautiful love, your compassionate heart, for all those times you showed up at the hospital with balloons and *that* smile, and for loving Kelly;

Joysa Maben Winter, for being my goddaughter, your special cookies and lemonade, sunflower seeds, mac and cheese, your stories, your love for me and Kelly, and for the ever-present source of joy that you are in my life;

My brothers Bill and Mike and their families for their love and support throughout the years;

the late Joseph E. White and the late Jennie D. White, my parents, for their ever present love then and now;

and finally, to my husband, John Martin, for your love and support throughout our life together. For being Kelly's *dad* and friend, for loving me before and after Kelly died, and for never giving up on me when I couldn't see a way out of the darkness of grief.

—*Jennifer J. Martin*

~

Entering the Labyrinth of Grief

~

"Making the decision to have a child—it's momentous.
It is to decide forever to have your heart go walking
around outside your body."
—Elizabeth Stone, quoted in *Village Voice* and *Reader's Digest* magazines,
teacher and author of *A Boy I Once Knew: What a Teacher Learned from
Her Student*

The Journey Begins

This book began when I decided to write the eulogy for my son's funeral. I was overwhelmed with what I was feeling, but managed, in the span of a few hours, in the darkness of the night, to give one last gift to him—or so I believed at the time.

Now it appears that this book may be the final gift, dedicated to his beautiful memory. Here is the writing that started it all:

A Eulogy for My Son, Kelly Hales
(August 26, 1967–February 5, 1991)

These thoughts are not intended to cause you sadness. They are to tell you of a beautiful life, a love story. What happened in Kelly's life is usually found in ancient fables that tell of a young hero's journey, a pawn turned into a knight.

On August 26, 1967, Kelly Wayne Hales was born into this world. He entered quietly, sent by God to teach us all many things.

When he was 4 years old, Kelly was diagnosed with mucopolysaccharidosis (or MPS), a congenital birth disorder that usually results in a myriad of bad things, including premature death.

Kelly was a precocious child and on one occasion, while being driven to nursery school, he advised his mother to "buy a piece of the rock" from Prudential Life Insurance. He must have seen the ad on television and felt compelled to offer his sage advice with a wisdom that exceeded his age but not his sensitivity—a trait he never lost.

Because of his physical handicaps, Kelly's teenage years were the hardest. This is a time when we leave childhood innocence and unconditional love for others and begin the unfortunate process of judging others and putting people in categories. Kelly managed to cope with it all and matured into a young man with a sense of great compassion and understanding, buoyed by a keen sense of humor.

Graduation from high school was a time of new beginnings for him—a time when Kelly began a spiritual journey. He knew he would have less time than most of us to complete his understanding of life, himself and of his personal relationship with God. Kelly's love became absolute and overwhelming. He learned in twenty-three years what it takes most of us a lifetime to learn. He accepted his mortality.

Two years prior to his death, Kelly was released from a hospital stay when we learned he was suffering from congestive heart failure. In the elevator the attendant stood behind Kelly, who was sitting in a wheelchair. The young man commented on what a beautiful day it was to be going home. Kelly replied, "Every day is a beautiful day."

Kelly found God in the final months of his time here. He read from his Bible and spiritual books, and volunteered in the Unity Church bookstore. He was in divine overdrive. He cherished the time he could spend with his family and beloved friends, and he honored every second of life.

For those of you who have seen the movie *Field of Dreams,* you will remember the voice that spoke and said, "If you build it, they will come." Kelly built the baseball diamond of his life in the innocence of knowing that people will come. And you have come today.

So if you have come to watch and experience this game we know as life, Kelly and I ask that you don't just sit in the bleachers and watch it pass you by. We ask that you participate in the game, that you honor your fellow players today, not tomorrow, and that you make a difference, as my son and best friend, Kelly Hales, did.

We love you all and we are so very honored that you could be here on this special day as you bear witness with us that Kelly's beautiful, incredible spirit outgrew his body and needed to fly. His blessing and ours is "God bless you and keep you forever in his care."

Lovingly,
Kelly's Mom, Jennifer

p.s. I have been preparing myself for this moment since Kelly was diagnosed with his illness. I hoped I would be ready and by the peace and grace of God and your love, I am.
p.p.s. Kelly's nickname was "Lucky."

◆   ◆   ◆

This eulogy and the writings that followed became a way for me to ease the pain in my heart. Putting words down on paper allowed me to acknowledge my grief and my love for my son. Through this process, I have found healing and been blessed to witness my own personal Easter, a resurrection of my very being from the depths of a loss that so devastated my life that I truly believed there would be no surviving such a tragedy.

Through this journey, I have found myself. And my hope is that you too may find *yourself*—perhaps for the very first time.

"The blissful sweet joy of your birth
The inconsolable sadness of your death
The depth of this sorrow—so unfathomable—dark and still
It engulfs me, washes over my bones, spirals past joyful memories of you
And with a thud, it lands in my heart—uninvited and unwanted grief."
—Jennifer J. Martin

The Screaming Room
February 5, 1991

"Your son may have suffered a stroke."

Those were the words from the nurse who called our home from the Medical Center Hospital in San Antonio, Texas. My husband, John, hurriedly drove us to the hospital. He dropped me off at the emergency room entrance while he parked the car.

Rushing inside, I discovered a throng of people seated and standing, all waiting for treatment for themselves or family members. After telling the receptionist who I was, she confirmed Kelly was in the emergency room and directed me to a small room down the hall, just outside the emergency room, where I should wait.

"A doctor will be out to talk with you in a minute," she said.

I found the private waiting room and was immediately struck by how hollow and sterile the space felt: blank walls, a small vinyl couch and two chairs, a metal trash can, a box of Kleenex. I took a seat on the edge of the black couch. Looking around, I thought it odd but very considerate of the clerk to allow us to wait in this room away from the crowd in the main lobby.

Moments later John appeared at the doorway of the small room, then sat beside me. He held my hand, and we talked quietly, speculating about how Kelly might be doing. Shortly, a small group of hospital personnel, all dressed in white, assembled at the door. I overheard one man whisper to the man standing next to him, "Someone said he was 35 or 40."

How odd. Who were these people talking about? It was a *Through the Looking Glass* kind of feeling.

Reality came into focus once again as the woman in front of the group began to speak. She introduced herself as the attending physician, asked if we were Kelly Hales' parents, then began to tell us of Kelly's condition upon his arrival at the hospital.

"His body was flaccid when the ambulance brought him in," she said. I didn't understand until later that this meant soft and limp.

He had been breathing, and they attempted to intubate him without success. They were forced to perform a tracheotomy to provide an airway. She continued to tell me details of the procedures they had performed when suddenly I realized she had not told us how Kelly was doing now.

My awareness was like the pause between breaths. Something was coming. It was coming next and it would expand and contract inside of me without my assistance. I was not in control. A silent knowing filled my soul.

"Is he gone?" I interrupted abruptly, cutting off the doctor in mid-sentence.

There was that split second of wavering between the dream and reality.

"Yes," she said softly.

My right leg began to spasm, bouncing up and down uncontrollably; my body convulsed and shook in disbelief. Sentences lined up behind my blank, staring eyes and exploded in my mind. *Oh my God, no. This can't be true. This isn't true. There must be some mistake. Kelly did not have a heart attack and die. My son is not dead.*

"I'm so sorry to tell you your son is dead," the doctor continued. "We did all we could to save him."

She asked me if I would like to see Kelly. I thought for a second, then declined. The sight of my dead son would give me no peace. I visualized him with a slit and bandaged throat. From all the past years of Kelly's surgeries and hospital stays, my mind was full enough of chafing visions, already a cognitive warehouse, stacked to the rafters of my brain: hospital corridors, swinging doors, snaking drainage tubes and beeping machines.

Suddenly, an old memory flooded my mind: the eerie *whoosh* of a respirator breathing for my son. A tear trickled down his face, my child, only 12 years old then, unable to speak to me of his needs.

"Are you in pain?" I had asked.

He shook his head.

"It's just all of this, isn't it?"

He nodded. Too much for a young man to endure, too much for his mother to watch.

Full enough was my hospital album of painful images. I didn't need to add another to my collection. I just wanted to remember him the way I saw him that morning, alive and smiling.

"If you change your mind, just let someone know," the attending physician said. Then, she turned away. The interns followed her, all disappearing behind the painted, metal swinging doors where I knew Kelly's body lay.

John and I sat there in shock, waiting. They had told us someone would be coming to speak with us about Kelly's belongings.

"Try to be calm," John said.

Inside, I felt dead.

John and I continued to wait in what we later learned was called the "screaming room." About twenty minutes later, a man in his mid-30s appeared at the door, wearing small gold-rimmed glasses. Speaking softly, he introduced himself as a representative from the organ donor program.

"Because of your son's small stature, his veins and heart arteries could be used for babies and young children," he told us.

He then said he would give us some time to think about it and would return shortly. Before he turned to leave, he also mentioned they could use Kelly's corneas for transplant.

Now alone, John and I talked about donating Kelly's veins and arteries. We concluded this would be something Kelly would want. He would want to help anyone he could, but especially children. Kelly adored children and had always wished he could have married and been a father.

By the time the man from the organ donor program returned, we had made our final decisions. We agreed to his initial request but declined the cornea tissue donation. These were my son's beautiful eyes, and I could not bear the thought of the procedure. The veins and arteries would have to be sufficient. I signed the papers, and the man thanked us for giving *the gift of life.*

Within a few minutes, the other papers concerning Kelly's belongings arrived. A phone call was received from his attending physician, indicating that an autopsy would not be required. The hospital staff informed us they would retrieve the tissue donations. Then Kelly's body would be taken to the funeral home.

John and I walked out of the automatic doors of the hospital and into the beginning of a sunset, probably one of the most beautiful I had ever seen. How could this be? John held onto me as we walked to the car, both of us still in shock. A day that began with a morning rainbow was coming to an end.

But another journey had already begun. It would lead me down a passageway to the belly of my soul, through meandering corridors illuminated by nothing but tears—a labyrinth of darkened chambered rooms where pieces of my shattered heart and soul now lay.

"I wish I could find something to make me as happy
as this has made me sad."

—Terry Osborne, bereaved parent
Forever Loved Support Group, 1994

<u>Beginning</u>
Feb. 6, 1991

For me, this journey begins with numbness and disbelief
followed by immense sorrow and heartache.
A rainbow marked the morning sky that day
But before sunset, I would become something else
A Bereaved Parent
I thought I was losing my mind
I thought I had lost my soul
that it had slipped free of my body
when they told me you were dead

"The light of a hundred stars does
not equal the light of the moon."
—Chinese Proverb

Healing Light
Feb. 8, 1991

Within a few days after Kelly's death but before the funeral, during a particularly sorrowful period, I awakened from a few minutes of restless sleep to find myself on my stomach. In my peripheral vision something appeared. I turned my head to see an image of a window floating in the air in the middle of my bedroom. The window resembled a fogged mirror or a window on a cold morning, clouded with condensation.

Then, as if someone were writing a message with an index finger, slowly, one letter at a time, words began to form on the windowpane revealing the message, *Because I love you.* As quickly as the window had appeared, it transformed into a ball of light, glowing white-hot, yet golden like a miniature sun.

Ever so slowly, the ball of light floated across the room toward me until the sphere was directly in front of me. It then penetrated my face between my eyes; the sensation was that of having a warm liquid poured into me, first coursing down my throat then expanding into my chest, flooding me with an intense heat. When the heat felt as if it had filled my entire chest cavity, it seemed to vaporize out through my back.

This was not my first encounter with a healing presence.

In 1971, following a week's hospitalization, when Kelly was 4, he was diagnosed with his illness. Our first night home, my young son slept on my bed as I sobbed uncontrollably. Suddenly I felt the weight of a hand upon my shoulder, as firm and real as if a person had touched me. But I was alone. When the pressure lifted, I heard a voice inside of me say, "Don't worry. He'll be okay. We'll take care of him."

To this day, I don't have any explanation for who wrote the message on the window. Was it Kelly, my guardian angel? The *who* doesn't seem to matter so much as the gift of receiving the healing energy. Whatever happened that night transformed my soul—it opened my heart and filled me up with grace and courage for the journey ahead.

"It is not true that we come here to live
We come only to sleep—to dream
All things are lent to us
We are only on earth in passing.
Tomorrow or the next day,
as you desire, Giver of life,
we shall go home to you."

—Guatemalan grief song

Feathers and a Funeral
Feb. 9, 1991

My older brother, Bill, and I believe in the beauty and mysticism of Native American spirituality and have each witnessed the healing that springs forth from practicing rituals. The day before the funeral, Bill arrived from Seattle with a gift for Kelly, two eagle feathers—feathers meant to help carry Kelly's spirit to heaven.

At the funeral home in the viewing room, we stood together before Kelly's casket. My brother asked where I wanted him to place the feathers. Since it was his gift to Kelly, I gave him permission to do whatever he wanted. I left him alone, standing over the casket, so he could perform his ceremony in privacy. I made my way to the far end of the visiting room where a few people sat talking. I watched as my brother closed his eyes and began to pray silently. Ever so slowly, he began to turn, stopping each time facing a new direction—north, south, east and west.

When Bill concluded his prayers, he returned to the casket. I waited a few minutes and then joined him. Gazing into the casket, I expected to see the feathers lying alongside Kelly's body. But they weren't there.

"Where did you put the feathers?" I asked him.

"I put them inside the sleeves of his jacket," he answered. "One beneath each arm."

I smiled. I remember feeling a sense of wonder and gratitude at my brother's act and also an understanding of great blessing for my son's spirit. Neither of us told anyone about the placement of the feathers. It was simply a sacred moment that had occurred between a brother and sister.

The next day was the funeral. The February air was crisp, the teal sky cloudless. There had been no wind that day. At the cemetery, immediately upon stepping from the family limousine, a gust of wind blew. The strong winds continued throughout the ceremony and didn't cease until the graveside service was over. Suddenly the air around me was calm. It was then I remembered having read something in an article about the ancients saying, "When a great soul dies, the winds go wild."

So perhaps the winds had assisted on carrying the great soul of my son to heaven. As I laid my hand on top of Kelly's closed coffin, a yellow butterfly landed on the floral arrangement atop the casket. Somewhere deep inside, I remembered that the butterfly is a symbol of renewal.

Following the funeral, everyone gathered at our home to share a meal. Most of Kelly's pallbearers had been close friends of his. One of the pallbearers, a young man named Ron, pulled me aside that afternoon.

"I need to tell you a dream I had about Kelly last night," he whispered.

I leaned in close to hear what he had to say.

"The dream was so strange," he continued. "I dreamed I saw God. God was standing before me like this." Ron gestured with both arms straight out from his sides, forming a human "T." He continued, "And God had these enormous wings like a bird's wings, only so big and beautiful."

Ron seemed to search for his next words. I waited for him to speak.

"And then that's when I saw him," Ron said.

"Saw who?"

"Kelly. I saw Kelly. He was tucked right here." Ron motioned with one hand, pointing his finger at the armpit of his still-outstretched limb. "That's where he was. Kelly was right there, tucked beneath God's wing."

In that instant, I made a connection between the eagle feathers my brother had placed in Kelly's jacket and the message I was receiving from Ron's dream. Tears fell from Ron's eyes as I shared the story.

"Kelly's safe now, home with God," Ron said, wiping at the tears that ran down his cheek.

Ron's dream served as a reminder of the miracle of life after death. God gave Ron that dream so he could give me a sign—a sign that my son's soul had made it safely home, with the aid of a brother's prayers, strong winds and two blessed eagle feathers.

"The ultimate goal of the grief work is to be able
to remember without emotional pain and to be able
to reinvest emotional surpluses. While the experience
of the grief work is difficult and slow and wearing,
it is also enriching and fulfilling.
The most beautiful people we have known are those who
have known defeat, known suffering, known struggle, known loss,
and have found their way out of the depths.
These persons have an appreciation, a sensitivity
and an understanding of life that fills them with
compassion, gentleness and a deep loving concern.
Beautiful people do not just happen."

—Elisabeth Kübler-Ross, MD
Death, The Final Stage of Growth

The Kindness of Strangers
March 20, 1991

Dear Dr. Belnick,

I am sorry it has taken me so long to write you. You may not remember me. I am Kelly Hales' mother. Kelly was the young man you cared for on February 5, 1991, at the emergency room of Medical Center Hospital. Kelly died that day.

I promised you I would mail a copy of Kelly's eulogy and so I have included a copy of same. The last few weeks and days have taught me so much about life. I am a volunteer for Santa Rosa Hospice and visit people who are dying from terminal illnesses. I decided to pursue this work so that I could learn about death, dying and grief in case I ever had to experience the loss of my son. I loved him so, that without this knowledge and experience, I doubt I would have survived losing him. But through the grace of God, family and friends, I have managed, so far, to continue to seek the peace that I know will come, and search for acceptance of the physical separation from my son.

Since all of this has happened, I have read a great deal of material on grief, death and dying, re-reading many of the Elizabeth Kubler-Ross books from my hospice volunteer training. After reading Kubler-Ross' books, I was reminded that people who work with death and dying are worthy of our compassion, for it is often hard and wearing. This caused me to become aware of my compassion for you. How difficult it must have been for you, a mother with children of your own, to tell me my son was dead. Your kindness will never be forgotten. I was blessed to have had you be the one to care for my son. I know you tried very hard to save his life.

As you might well imagine, throughout Kelly's life we experienced many clinical, cold physicians, who always made our journey more painful. I will forever remember your words to me following Kelly's death, expressing how much love and care it must have taken to allow him to live this long with his degree of physical problems.

If I could have, I would have struck a deal with God on that day. I would have exchanged my life and physical health so my son could live. I told my husband shortly after Kelly died that I thought God should give you choices—that when it is time for someone you dearly love to leave this earth, that God should give you the option to go with them, if you so choose. I would have opted to die with Kelly on that day, for he was my best friend, my teacher, my forever companion and my son.

Often in this life, we are blessed to live with great souls. I was blessed to live with a great spirit for twenty-three years. You only knew him for an instant, but he touched you and the great aspect of your beautiful soul touched him and our family. Thank you for your tender compassion.

Love and Best Wishes,
Jennifer J. Martin

"Remember that pain has this most excellent quality:
if prolonged it cannot be severe,
and if severe it cannot be prolonged."

—Epistulae ad Lucilium, XCIV
Roman author and statesman
Seneca (circa 4 BC–AD 65)

First Birthday
August 22, 1991

I feel the need to write tonight. Your birthday is approaching in four days. For the first time, I won't be going to the store to buy you that special card and find that perfect gift. Instead, I will visit your grave and take flowers, maybe buy some balloons with long ribbons. One balloon will say "I Love You." Another, "Happy Birthday." I will tether the balloons to the bronze vase atop your grave and wait until the breeze comes and catches and drops them, tapping and bumping against your headstone. There is always a breeze at your grave.

I remember your last birthday. I made your favorite lasagna. Grandma and Grandpa came. You were so happy.

In my heart, I know you know the abounding love I wish to give to you today and on your birthday. You have always been my heart, my dearest and sweetest love. I treasured your presence in my life for the pure light that you were. To see your smile or hear your laughter today would so lighten my heart.

I miss you so terribly. I find myself suppressing my grief, and I feel so very guilty for occupying my mind with almost anything to not feel the pain of missing you. I don't want to live to be old, because I don't want to live apart from you. I wish I could have gone with you on that day. It would have been a simultaneous release of two souls departing as one. You mirrored my soul and now the mirror is broken. I have no reflection.

"In her mind's eye, it was Christmas before last once again, when she stood in this very spot, her arms wrapped tightly around Taylor to prevent him from falling over the edge of the balcony. That day he wore his little red bathing suit and stood barefoot on the flat, low edge of the stucco wall that faced the ocean. Only this time, he didn't squeal with delight or point to the sailboats in the harbor. Julia just held him tight and breathed in the sweet memory of her son."

—Jennifer J. Martin
Heaven's Stone

Christmas
December 2, 1991

I find the books I read a month ago that soothed my mind and heart and gave me such a feeling of peace are now but a memory. Now I need a new salve for another wound—one I didn't anticipate in the early weeks of November: the holidays.

Radio, TV and newspaper ads all speak to the hearts of those who care that it's Christmas. They don't speak to me.

The first holidays following the death of a child feel the same as the days following the child's death, when we were so astonished that the world could continue in any normal fashion. We thought it incomprehensible. Our world had collapsed. How could theirs continue? But then as the weeks go by, you begin to understand, not necessarily accept, but understand why the world goes on. And you also don't long to be a part of it yet. It's too soon.

I don't long to be a part of this first Christmas, but rather wish I could go to a place where there is no Christmas, a place that has no memory of the last twenty-three Christmases. I'd like to find a place where I can go to sleep in the latter weeks of November—and awaken after January 2. A place to forget my pain.

It would be a place where angels would unfold my heart with hands more tender than a mother's, and in that sacred space where my heart has been broken, they would instill a sense of acceptance and peace.

There, the healing angels would whisper softly to me, saying: "Take all the time you need to heal. Be gentle with yourself. We'll be here as long as you need us."

"The eyes are the mirror of the soul."
—Philippine proverb

Mirror of the Soul
March 24, 1992

Blond, graying hair, azure-blue eyes, auburn hair, watercolor-green eyes, raven-black hair, irises of eyes the color of polished mahogany—all empty eyes staring at me. Eyes that are sad and haunting, some glistening with the onset of tears, all mirroring the woundedness of shattered lives and hearts.

I remember the first time I attended the Forever Loved support group for bereaved parents. Attempting to follow directions to the meeting room, given to me by the church secretary, I took a nearby stairway and continued down a hall. There I passed a woman. When our eyes met, I knew she was a bereaved parent. A fleeting, faint smile faded from her face as quickly as it had appeared. In her eyes I saw my own mirrored reflection, which expressed a soul ripped open, eyes staring off to a secret place of knowing or not knowing, of asking a thousand *whys*, or asking *why me, why my child*? Eyes fixed on the floor or a place on the wall, seeking and finding a void.

We sit here now, parents who have buried children. In this tiny circle, this sacred space, a place where we will come once a week to utter our child's name and tell their/our story, stories of a child's death caused by murder, illness, suicide or accident but all tales with the same ending—a chronicle of events that does not end with "and they lived happily ever after."

In the span of an hour or so, stories will be told, most accompanied by tears. A grown woman seated on the couch next to another mother will curl up, childlike, and rest her head on the other woman's shoulder. The other woman will hold her while she is allowed to weep uncontrollably. Her son was murdered. Then a father will express his rage at his son's death, another dad will struggle with the guilt that haunts him.

We all understand the feelings—the longing and the pain. There will be those few who cannot speak. Their silence is accepted. They come only to listen, to begin to heal themselves by listening to our stories. Ultimately, we are all here to learn we are not going crazy, to begin to believe that with tears wept and stories told again and again, this pain we now feel will someday and somehow rest softer against our souls.

During the course of the meeting, in the midst of the sadness, someone's fleeting happy memory will surface and a *before* story of a child will be told. There will be smiles and even laughter and for one cherished instant, eyes that appeared flat and unanimated will twinkle, mirroring joy-filled hearts that also remember. In closing, a prayer is offered up. We will share long hugs and make a promise to come back as often as we can, to sit in this sacred circle until we are able to walk out the door when more joy than pain is remembered, until that day when we each will become a wounded healer.

A new mother is here tonight. Her teenage son committed suicide two weeks ago. The pain reflected in her eyes and heart—inconsolable.

How I remember the ache of that sorrow. How searing the blade of anguish was in my gut. I consider the loss of a child to suicide or murder to be particularly hard to bear. It's a grief with harder edges, more corners. Simply, more of everything that is painful. After hearing about parents' losses due to murder and suicide, Kelly's death due to illness seemed somehow softer to embrace.

I am thankful to no longer be in the grasp of the early devastation. I will always be grateful for the presence of numbness in the early days. Otherwise, how would we survive? The remembrance of waking the night after Kelly's death to a vision of a woman in the mirror—me—with eyes so swollen from crying that a view of the world seemed impossible.

Who was this woman who now walked the floors of my house at night with no understanding of where she was or even a concern about where she might be? Who was this woman incapable of dressing to go to the funeral home to discuss arrangements for the burial of her child? How does one dress for such an occasion?

I remember asking that question of the sad woman in the mirror staring back at me.

"The soul would have no rainbow
if the eyes had no tears."

—Minquass Proverb

Sorrow and Tears
April 20, 1992

I try to continue to repress the pain but sometimes I must allow the sorrow and tears to enter—in order to feel the tremendous love once again. Tonight I am writing left-handed on yellow-lined paper. Someone said that writing in this way helps express the pain on some childlike level. I can hardly make out the words. They are large and resemble the scribbling of a young child.

This is what I wrote:

I am so sad. I need to express to the world how sad I feel. No one understands how much I hurt. Not true. I do have friends who understand. I am grateful. Kelly, my best friend, my son. I love you so much. I miss you! Please, God, help me to see my friend, my love, my son again. I pray for this.

"In the house with the tortoise chair
she will give birth to the pearl
to the beautiful feather

in the house of the goddess who sits on a tortoise
she will give birth to the necklace of pearls
to the beautiful feathers we are

there she sits on the tortoise
swelling to give us birth

on your way on your way
child be on your way to me here
you whom I made new
come here child come be pearl
come be feather."

—Aztec prayer
Jerome Rothenberg, *Shaking the Pumpkin: Traditional Poetry
of the Indian North Americas.* (English version by Anselm Hollo)

Mother's Day
May 10, 1992

As I write on this day, I am feeling somewhat distant from the people who will visit our house later today. I couldn't bear the thought of going to church. Some stranger standing at the entrance passing out red carnations to the women. Later, the usual recognition of the youngest and the oldest mothers in attendance. Would they have a flower and a special acknowledgment for the saddest mother?

No thanks. I learned my lesson the hard way the first Mother's Day. The reminders of the upcoming event were everywhere—at the grocery store, on television commercials. At the drug store, large cardboard banners, colored pink and white, bordered with photographs of flower bouquets, announce: Mother's Day Cards. Yes, here they are: To Mother With Love, From Your Son.

The first Mother's Day, I sidestepped it all. No going to church for me, or even seeing my own mother on that day. The sabotage happened at a coffee shop. Innocently enough, the cashier smiled at me from behind the cash register and wished me a Happy Mother's Day. She never felt the pain in my heart caused by her greeting, nor did she see me crying on the way to my car.

This is the second Mother's Day. Friends and family who visit today are well intentioned. They hug me and wish me a Happy Mother's Day. One brings me a pot of orange mums and a card, and whispers in my ear, "You're still a mother." But inside of my aching heart it doesn't feel that way, just lonely and sad. How can I still be a mother when my child is dead?

I just want to be alone with my thoughts and music, to capture these words on paper as they pass over my heart. Thoughts of motherhood and a pregnancy, prior to my being pregnant with Kelly, haunted me in the days preceding today. I was as joyous about the first pregnancy as I was with Kelly. Maternal instinct told me perhaps this first baby would be a girl. I so longed for a little daughter.

But early in the pregnancy I was exposed to the German measles. Doctors advised me there was an eighty percent chance the baby would be born blind, deaf or brain damaged. I simply could not endure the thought of bringing a child into the world with those difficulties, not for my sake. It just did not seem fair to the baby.

It was 1965 and abortions were not an everyday occurrence. My husband was in the Navy and the base hospital did not perform abortions. I was forced to see two civilian doctors who signed documentation that confirmed I did have the German measles. This was the first step to allow for a therapeutic abortion to be performed. Once again I was given the grim prognosis of this baby being born with severe defects.

The choice was mine and with the consent of my husband, I elected to terminate this birth. I struggled with the decision, but, ultimately, it was with the greatest of love that I released this child back to the heavens. I always felt this baby was a little girl—a knowingness that cannot be explained. Even after Kelly's birth, I longed for this little girl.

In 1987, I attended a weekend workshop that altered my life. Held at a friend's home, the group was intimate, a total of twelve men and women. We followed guided meditations, listened to music and shared our experiences from the meditations. Throughout most of the weekend, I found myself crying, thinking about the abortion. I never shared the reason for my tears with any of those at the workshop, and no one asked. Everyone in attendance was experiencing and clearing very emotional life issues, and tears just seemed to be a part of that process.

At one point in the workshop, we were all focused on opening our hearts to allow for unconditional love to both fill us up and flow outward to others. During the heart-opening exercise, each participant sat on the carpeted floor with eyes closed. As the facilitator passed through the group, he stopped behind each participant and placed an amethyst crystal at his or her back behind the heart and a clear crystal over the heart.

I recall feeling something profound had occurred when the facilitator stopped behind me, and because of this feeling, I requested a private meeting with him the following week. We met on a Monday morning. I told him about the sense of something significant happening when he paused behind me during the heart meditation and asked if he recalled anything about that moment.

He replied, "Have you ever had an abortion?"

In total shock, because I had not shared this with anyone in the group, including him, I burst into tears. I explained the circumstances surrounding the abortion so many years ago. I also told him I always hoped I had done the right thing for this baby.

He spoke with great calm, "I don't know why, but I thought you'd had an abortion. As I stopped behind you, I saw a little golden-haired girl. She was speaking to you, although you could not hear her words. She said, 'I cannot hold your hand, but I will forever embrace your heart.' She merely wanted to tell you that she loved you and that, yes, you did do the right thing."

In the weeks that followed, I knew I finally had my little golden-haired daughter. I named her Sarah. (I have since learned that this name in Hebrew means *noble* or *princess*.) If only in spirit, Sarah was my child and she had been with me always. So now I have two children of spirit, Kelly and Sarah.

Come little girl of my heart, my pearl, my feather, and place your tiny hand in mine—my princess.

"The Lord has given me many mountains to climb in my lifetime, but this time I'm too old, it's too steep and he left me no shoes."

—Bill Bullard, Michael Benishek's grandfather,
on learning of his grandson's murder

Mate

May 20, 1992

Grandpa had another heart attack today. I remember when you were still here, once a week you'd go pick him up, take him to lunch and spend the day with him to give Grandma White a little break—a few hours of reprieve from caring for him.

I remember your Grandpa always called us both "Mate," the Navy version of *friend*. You called him Mate as well. I remember we both always thought this very odd, since he was a staunch career Army man.

I remember at your funeral Grandma White didn't want Grandpa to attend. He'd suffered several mild heart attacks at the last funerals of friends he had attended. I recall Grandpa White saying, "If you don't let me go—it will kill me." When he saw you for the first time, lying in the casket, through tear-filled eyes, he whispered to you, "Wait for me at the gate, Mate."

"The grief could only end if a place could be found for it to begin."

—Molly Fumia
A Child at Dawn, The Healing of a Memory

Wet Pain
May 29, 1992

The wetness of this pain lies against me, heavy, clinging and cold, as if someone forgot and left my soul out in the rain.

"You can't even imagine the pain." That's what I say to people who have never lost a child. They shake their head, avert their eyes and quietly reply, "No, you're right. I can't even imagine what it would feel like."

I recall my goddaughter Joysa's words to me after Kelly died: "I sit and I think. What can I do to help you? You're just so sad. I think to myself, how can I make you feel better? If only you could forget. That would make you feel better. But then I pause and say, No, I would never want you to forget, never. I would never want to take your memories away."

Somewhere, somehow, in the midst of the sorrow, I am able to remember the love, which in the end is the reason for all of this pain in my heart. Then, I do it again. I bend down, pick them up, dust them off, all the pieces of my broken heart. Once again I have transcended that broken place inside of me. Once again I will invite life inside my heart. Once again, I will always be grateful to have known a love this big, even in the midst of the storm.

Thankful for twenty-three years of a love this deep. Very thankful.

"Both boy and man was he,
yet neither.
The vastness of his being
could not be contained
in a physical form.
He came to warm the hearts of others,
to decant his ancientness
into a world of duality and confusion.

And though met with judgment
time and time again,
he offered his love
with the purity and mercy of a Bodhisattva.
Ageless radiance
poured through his eyes."

—Rashani
(Written for Kelly)

Old Soul
July 16, 1992

When I tell strangers you were 23 when you died, they assume you were allowed to experience the world fully, in all the aspects a young man might during a normal life, just one halted too soon. But because they didn't know you, they fail to comprehend that, because of your birth defects, you left this world with a body resembling a 12-year-old.

So, how do I bury the body of a 12-year-old, which is, in reality, the body and soul of a grown man? It occurs in the privacy and grace of having known you. If only they had—those strangers who used to stare at you and wonder, *Is he a child or a man?*

So, have I buried my young child or a grown young man?

Neither.

I have buried a very old soul. One had only to look into your eyes to know the soul that resided within was ancient and forever knowing. You were neither child nor adult. You existed beyond either purpose. You were a teacher who came bearing witness to God's infinite wisdom in placing special beings in our midst.

You died because your soul outgrew your body and needed to fly.

"One often calms one's grief by recounting it."

—Pierre Corneille (1606–1684)
French dramatist
Polyeucte, I:3

Chinese and Russian
August 25, 1992

It had been eighteen months since Kelly had died. Somewhere around this time I remember feeling that my husband, John, Kelly's stepfather, was not supporting me in my grief process. He was angry and had become increasingly critical of my sadness and grieving. He, like so many others, thought it was time to move on.

I was angry at John for a lot of reasons—for changing the subject whenever I needed to talk about Kelly, for leaving the room if I started to cry, for not holding me when I needed him. My needs were as endless as the sorrow I felt. I was like a child—a motherless child who could find no one to comfort her.

I knew John and I needed to talk to somebody about what was going on with us. Our relationship and our marriage were at stake. John agreed, and I made an appointment with a grief therapist through a program called Someone's Listening.

The therapist's question was a simple one: "How do you react when someone you love dies?"

I responded immediately. "Well, it helps me if I can talk about it, cry about it and sometimes write about it."

Then it was my husband's turn. "Loss is just something you have to accept," he said.

John had recently lost his mother and a sister. "There's nothing I can do to change the situation," he continued, "and I simply feel I have to move on."

The counselor said he understood why we were having problems in the grief process.

He said, "You see, John, it's as if Jennifer only understands Chinese and you are speaking Russian."

This simple sentence was an immense lesson to me in how people grieve differently.

At a later time, a social worker who worked for a local hospice shared another viewpoint on grief. We talked about the different ways people grieve.

She said, "If grief is an ocean, there are people who will stand with their backs to it. They can feel the ocean breeze in their hair and on their face, smell the salt air, feel the surf lapping at their feet and ankles. But they can't face the ocean. But every now and then a big wave will come and it will wash over them, soak their clothing, maybe even knock them over. And in those moments, they will have to deal with grief, face the pain of their loss."

My response was simple. "Me, I'd just walk into the ocean," I said. "That's the only way I know how to deal with loss. Immerse myself in the grief. Feel it all."

In *my* understanding of this healing process, power is established in feeling. Not for everyone but for me and people like me. I would not change for one moment the emotions I am capable of feeling.

I could never turn my back on the ocean. I would fall to my knees in the sand, close my eyes and pray for that first wave to crash over me, to soak my body with pain. I would scream my son's name—louder than the ocean's roar—shiver in the coldness of death and wait for the healing that would finally come.

The Seed I Keep

Do not the bitter seed spit out,
nor curse the raging rain.
Throw not the sour wine away,
or flee from trying pain.
For suffering lends compassion,
and tears, deep empathy,
and those who've lived
through darkest hours...
best comfort those who weep.

—Deborah Lindsay O'Toole

A Knowing Touch
September 17, 1992

One can more truly comfort pain that one can understand. If a hand reaches out to me and it knows not the pain within my heart, I sense that. Though grateful for the love and kindness extended, I long for the depth of compassion from the hand of one who *knows*. For they know my heart. It is their heart as well.

They have buried a child. They have gazed at their child's face and said goodbye forever. They have cried rivers of tears. They will sit with me through the darkness of this pain. They are my brothers and my sisters. They are my family, not of the same blood, but of the same shared-soul experience—my family of the heart.

"Nothing so smooth as the side of a thorn,
Nothing so calm as the eye of a storm."

From the song "Go To The Water"
by Kat Eggleston on *Outside Eden*

Letting Go
October 8, 1992

It's been twenty months since your death and I find myself doing something I never thought I would ever do—suppressing thoughts of you. There has been so much pain, and I miss you so. I put away your shoes in a drawer, and I moved your heart medication from the kitchen shelf to your closet and placed them in a basket with your folded shirts. I wasn't strong enough to throw out your medicine. Somehow I feel it still keeps me connected to you. When I picked up the bottles of pills, I hesitated. A part of me wanted to keep them there, but the part of me that has grown said, *No, it is time to start letting go.* I don't want to let go, but I know that to survive I must begin.

September 22 was the fall solstice—a new beginning. I remember feeling a new liveliness following that day, the sort of energy required to clean out closets, wash the baseboards and rearrange furniture. I rearranged your bedroom. When I was finished, I thought you would approve.

I made a decision about the disposition of your clothes that same day. I can't do it today but when I'm stronger I will donate them all to young boys living on the Indian reservation in Taos. I thought you would like that.

"To pass through a thicket, you have to rely on shoes."

—African Proverb (Shona)

Our Children's Shoes
March 8, 1992

Shoes, a toothbrush, a pair of eye glasses, a bathrobe, a prescription bottle of heart medication, a favorite box of cereal, a blue and yellow box of Kraft macaroni and cheese. All little reminders of the emptiness that fills the rooms of my home and my heart.

I never viewed a pair of shoes sitting empty on the floor as a representation of life or as a reminder of a life that used to be. Shoes are something we take for granted in our world. Even people who can't walk wear shoes. We choose a pair each morning according to our mood and schedule and think little of how they carry us through the day. They provide balance and support for our bodies and protect our feet from injury. And it was the one item of clothing the funeral director told me not to bring. "Bring socks, but no shoes," he said.

Now a pair of burgundy corduroy house slippers represents memories of mornings, sunshine, coffee and wonderful discussions at the breakfast table. The slippers sit motionless in a closet upstairs resting beneath a hanging navy bathrobe that once accompanied the slippers on those early mornings and late nights when comfort was required.

A pair of gray Italian dress shoes represents a once happier time and a time of feeling good. Those same shoes are now scuffed on the sides from the asphalt where you lay dying, or perhaps scuffed when that kind person pulled you from your car and tried to save you. These gray Italian shoes were the same ones a hospital worker handed me, sealed in a plastic bag along with your blood-stained, plaid shirt (cut open with scissors in the emergency room), your glasses, a set of car keys and your wallet filled with cash, an ATM receipt showing a withdrawal of forty dollars at 14:14 p.m. I held that receipt in my hand as if it were a lifeline to your last moments of being alive: 2:14, still here. One hour and twelve minutes later that day at 3:26 p.m. you would be pronounced dead, and my world would never be the same.

Objects all: shoes, a shirt, glasses, keys, wallet, an ATM receipt, once your things, now sad things that echo the emptiness of your absence. It matters not whether the size of the shoe fits tiny within the palm of our hand or was allowed the time to grow into an adult size. We will always wish that the shoes could have supported that life longer, could have worn out from use and had to be replaced with something new. We will always wish that our children would need their shoes.

"Heavy hearts, like heavy clouds in the sky,
are best relieved by the letting of a little water."

—Antoine Rivarol (1792–1868)
Italian opera composer

An Empty Sky
April 7, 1992

I sit in the green, overstuffed chair, staring through the wavy glass windows of my Victorian house. My arms curl around knees pulled to my chest. Sometimes when the tears fill my eyes, I think I feel God. A sacred moment. Sometimes I confuse God and love. I really shouldn't, because they're the same.

I sit here and wonder: How can the world go on? Doesn't the world know my child has died? How can the world be ordered any longer? The sight of the scheduled UPS truck driving down my street becomes a symbol of madness. My universe no longer exists—an empty sky with no sun, no moon, no stars.

Let it be before. Before the rockslide of my life; before I labeled grief a harsh mistress; before when a child's death was some dark abstraction, not a grim reality; before grief became the black, dark pain in my heart and soul; before my son died and my heart was broken. Please let it be before, when, in a tiny crevice of my heart, only fragile things resided. Nothing broken there, no shattered shards of a soul, only magic. But that was before—before February 5, 1991, at 3:26 p.m.

And yet the world does go on, without me, without my son. Somehow, someday it has to be okay—I think and pray. Grace will find me and allow me to go on, to go on without him, not just to survive but to live fully and joyfully.

A loss such as this rips us open. As one bereaved mother, Jane Mowrey, said to me following the death of her 7-year-old son, Michael, to cancer: "You can either lie down or fly."

"When you are sorrowful look again in your heart,
and you shall see that in truth you are weeping
for that which has been your delight."

—Kahlil Gibran
The Prophet

A January Night
May 19, 1992

A January night—it's almost like a dream—a dream that you're not here with me. It just seems so unreal that you have gone from this house. I remember your deep contagious laughter, your sparkling soulful eyes. The only images of you I will ever see again is captured in the stillness of photographs. Your voice and laughter now silent. Never again will you walk into this room. Never again will I know the joy of your physical presence.

When I hear the rain now, I always open the French doors to the deck and listen intently. I remember you said one night how much you loved the sound of rain. Sometimes, late in the evening, when I'm sitting alone in the kitchen, I pull your chair out, the one you always sat in. I invite you to come and sit with me and talk or watch late night shows (like we used to do). You remember, don't you son?

The finish on the old oak kitchen chair is worn off from where you used to stand with elbows resting on the top. I hate it when other people sit in your chair. I hate it because if you were still here, you would be sitting, standing or leaning on it. I always knew that you used to stand and lean over your chair because it allowed you to breathe easier. For comfort and balance, you would always cross one foot over the other, while standing. Other people would be uncomfortable in this position, but for you, because of your small stature, it was a perfect resting place.

This kitchen holds so many memories of you. Almost all the memories of our last week together were made in this room. It was a cold morning, in late January, when you walked into the kitchen. I was sitting at the kitchen table having my coffee. You wore your blue and burgundy bathrobe, and corduroy house shoes. As you poured yourself some juice, I told you that your ankles looked swollen.

You said, "Mom, you need to keep a better eye on me." You called and made an appointment to see your doctor. I recall the day you went to your appointment. I felt I should have gone with you, but you assured me that you could handle it on your own. I became concerned when you had been gone for quite a while. When you finally came home, you told me that the doctor had doubled your heart medication and your diuretics. You also said that if the swelling didn't go down, the doctor had recommended you see a cardiologist. My heart grew sick at the sound of your words.

That night, you asked me if I would prepare a foot bath for you in hopes it would ease the swelling. I remember carrying a plastic yellow tub upstairs to your room. I found you sitting in the small apple-green rocking chair. I prepared your bath, putting some healing oils into the water and testing the temperature of the water to ensure that it was not too hot. I placed the footbath in front of your chair. You gingerly immersed your swollen feet and ankles beneath the soothing water. You said, "Ah." Shortly you asked me to refill the water and as you soaked your feet in the second mixture, you told me your ankles and feet felt better.

Before I tossed the water, I moved the tub to the side and gathered a small towel around each foot. I tenderly dried each foot, one at a time. As I was kneeling before you, I raised my head and looked into your eyes. You smiled and said not a word.

In that brief moment, I knew you had evolved into the most beautiful soul I had ever known. You had transcended every tragedy in your young life and there was a peace that surrounded you that I longed to comprehend. I felt for one fleeting moment that I seen the face of God. For in your eyes, I was blessed to behold the essence of your benevolent soul.

You died one week later.

"It is such a secret place, the land of tears."

—Antoine de Saint-Exupéry
The Little Prince

Emptiness
July 18, 1992

Sometimes I accept and understand that you're gone, and for days, even a few weeks, it's okay that you're in a special place. Then there come those hours, days and weeks when the emptiness of the hole left in my world reaches beyond any time that may be measured by the ticking of a clock. There are so many days and nights when your absence is unbearable.

There is not a being, not one, who is capable of nourishing my soul as you did—with the warmth of your contagious laughter, the tenderness of your smile and your ever-constant companionship. My God, how I miss you.

I ache for the sound of your voice, our sharing of the day we each experienced and your sage advice about this old world. I hope that in heaven you don't miss me the way I miss you here. I'm sure God has special angels who help you with that.

Two days ago (on my birthday), I went to the Lourde's Grotto and gave thanks for my life and for the gift of knowing a love such as yours for twenty-three years. I forgot to ask God to not let me miss you so much. I guess it was one of those *better* days when I offered up that prayer and lit the candle for you and for me. I forgot to ask God to take the emptiness away.

"While grief enters the house as a stranger,
it often leaves as a friend.
A messenger who brings unwanted news,
grief stays to endure our disbelief,
and to instruct us in the healing
art of profound acceptance."

—Molly Fumia
Safe Passage, Words to Help the Grieving

Angel in My Midst
September 13, 1993

Oh God, I have lost so much.

Kelly, you were my forever companion. I never knew how long I would have you, but my daily heart prayer was that you would be that *one statistic* who defied the odds of a shortened life, of a birth defect, of a missing chromosome. Be that one, for me. Please, be that one.

Then, on a sunny afternoon in February, you suddenly died. Now everything we shared with one another was ripped from my midst, instantly and forever gone. My world and heart shattered by the nod of a physician's head to my one question: *Is he gone?*

What were you to me? You were my breath on the mirror, my infinite deep pool of joy, tenderness, love, laughter and wisdom. You were my past and my future, sunrise and sunset, my heart and soul reflected.

You were the memory of a baby's face framed by golden curls and sea glass eyes; a little plastic frog named Kermit with a Santa hat that once held your Christmas stocking; tanned golden-brown summer skin, sun-bleached hair; a treasured red bicycle; and a little black dog named Radar.

You were the rain in the desert, the pearl in the oyster, the flicker of a candle, the whisper in the wind, the ocean's roar in a sea shell, the bubbles in a glass of champagne. You were the sun glistening off a vein of spider's eggs I found hidden beneath a leaf blade one morning in the garden.

You were my only child, my son, my everything.

Now, you are the ache in my heart from staggering loss; you are tears, pain and longing; you are the silence of the graveyard as the Mylar balloon that reads "Happy Birthday" is caught by the wind, and bumps and taps against your headstone.

I am grateful for having borne a soul such as yours—a great, expansive, compassionate being, beyond understanding—an angel in my midst. I thank God for the deepening of my soul, for the lesson of compassion and for the enormous love that I have known in the gift of being your mother and your friend.

"When sorrow comes, let us accept it simply, as a part of life.
Let the heart be open to pain; let it be stretched by it.
All the evidence we have says that this is the better way
…And in the process will come a deepening inward knowledge
that in the final reckoning, all is well."
—A. Powell Davies
Great Occasions: Readings for the Celebration of Birth,
Coming of Age, Marriage and Death

Let's Not Talk About It
February 5, 1994

Today is the third anniversary of your death. I remember. Does anyone else? I doubt it. Your grandma told me she took flowers to the cemetery today, then quickly changed the subject to who came by for a visit or any other topic so we wouldn't have to talk about what today really is—the day you died, three years ago.

I watched for the mail today, and was glad when it came early. But there were no cards remembering your death. There *were* cards for the first two years. I guess by the third year, no one feels it's necessary to remember. Perhaps they believe that surely everything must be okay now. The pain is all gone. If they only knew the power and the love felt in receiving just one card—a token of remembrance. If they only knew…

Yes, everyone is busying themselves today, thinking other thoughts, anything to distract themselves from this day. How very sad that we do not have the learned capacity to acknowledge our loss and our pain.

We don't have the social skills to be able to communicate our needs to one another because everyone seems to be running from their own fear of grief and loss. How very sad.

"Only when you drink from the river of silence shall you indeed sing. And when you have reached the mountaintop, then shall you begin to climb. And when the earth shall claim your limbs, then shall you truly dance."

—Kahlil Gibran
The Prophet

A Place Called Grace
January 11, 1995

Grief is a harsh mistress—I was determined to face her. She was the dark pain in my heart. With all my courage, I invited her in, holding her close in an embrace, allowing the grief to penetrate my soul. In the beginning I danced with her in silence, no music, no lyrics.

Then I lanced my own soul wound and welcomed the pain, knowing there was no greater suffering than the day I buried my son. In the exhausting darkness of the night, I lit candles and consciously listened to music—songs like "Fragile" on Sting's album *Nothing Like the Sun*, and "If I Had Only Known" on Reba McEntire's album *For My Broken Heart*.

The music evoked memories, both precious and sad, until the tears came, always silent, but hot and full.

Often I wrote in my journal, attempting to make sense of the dark abstraction of death and searching for the words to describe the joy, life and laughter that was taken from me. I deliberately emptied my heart of the tears that I knew must be shed to facilitate my healing. Without my asking, God held me tightly in the night and sent angels to dry my tears with the most tender brush of their silent wings.

The lyrics of "If I Had Only Known," written by Jana Stanfield and Craig Morris, were soulfully prophetic the first time I heard them and each time thereafter. Every time I listened to the song, my heart was emptied of the sorrow I was feeling in that moment.

"If I Had Only Known"

If I had only known
It was the last walk in the rain
I'd keep you out for hours in the storm
I would hold your hand
Like a life line to my heart
Underneath the thunder we'd be warm
If I had only known
It was our last walk in the rain

If I had only known
I'd never hear your voice again
I'd memorize each thing you ever said
And on those lonely nights

I could think of them once more
Keep your words alive inside my head
If I had only known
I'd never hear your voice again

You were the treasure in my hand
You were the one who always stood
beside me
So unaware I foolishly believed
That you would always be there
But then there came a day
And I turned my head and you
slipped away

If I had only known
It was my last night by your side

I'd pray a miracle would stop the dawn
And when you'd smile at me
I would look into your eyes
And make sure you know my love
For you goes on and on
If I had only known
If I had only known
The love I would've shown
If I had only known

"If you ever lose a child the way I did, then you'll know the other side of the truth. You'll understand what it means to be destroyed and still get up every day and fill the kettle with water. You will see steam from the kettle and weep. Insist nothing is wrong. A piece of dirt flew up and lodged beneath your eyelid. That's all. On the street, tears will fall onto the sidewalk and fill up your shoes. Say the sun is in your eye. Maybe you have pinkeye. If you show your grief, it won't go away. It is with you forever, and ever, but there may be an hour when you don't remember. An evening when the sky is blue as ink. An afternoon when your daughter runs after a cricket she will never catch. Whisper your baby's name. Then be quiet. If you're lucky, you'll hear the name said back to you every time you close your eyes."

—Alice Hoffman
"Advice from my Grandmother" in *Family, American Writers Remember Their Own*

A Single Blue Sock
May 17, 1996

In the Forever Loved support group, Nancy was one of the parents who always shared openly, grieved deeply and cried a lot. Both initially and every time she shared her story, the immensity of her sorrow always touched me deeply.

Tonight at the meeting of Forever Loved, Nancy was crying. It had been five years since her 4½-year-old son, Heath, had been hit by a car and killed. But tonight Nancy was crying about something else. Something simple. She was crying about a single blue sock, Heath's sock—the one she found behind her dryer when she moved it out from the wall. That's all, just a sock, a single blue sock that belonged to a little boy named Heath.

"Absence is to love what wind is to fire; it extinguishes the small, it inflames the great."

—Bussy-Rabutin (Roger de Rabutin, Comte de Bussy; 1618–1693)
French soldier and writer
Histoire amoureuse des Gaules

The Hurting
June 10, 1997

"When will I stop hurting?" I asked my brother Bill after a love relationship ended painfully years earlier in my youth, many years before the death of my son.

My brother replied, "Whenever you're done with it."

The death of a child is the ultimate loss, deeper and greater than the loss of a romantic love. It would take longer, much longer, *years* for this pain to leave me.

My lover existed before I did, not because of me. My lover did not die; he just went away. I did not give birth to him. He didn't have my eyes or my sense of humor. He didn't share my soul—or take it with him when he left.

~

Emerging from the Other Side

~

"And he took me by the hand, but he was still worrying.
'It will look as if I were dead; and that will not be true…'. I said nothing.
'You understand…it is so far. I cannot carry this body with me.
It is too heavy. But it is like an old abandoned shell.
There is nothing sad about shells.'"

—Antoine de Saint-Exupéry
The Little Prince

Purpose
January 16, 1992

If I begin to understand life purposes, then you completed all of your lessons, son. The lessons of living in a compromised body and the knowledge, in the end, that you were truly loved and valued by so many people who met you—that they would know love and healing from your presence.

My lessons continue. I am still here on earth. I came to be your mother and to learn about overcoming the tragedy of your death and to understand that the memory of the love we share is great enough to sustain and heal me. For nobody loved me like you did, nor did I love anyone more than I loved you.

I am here to share one final lesson with others—to write of the peace I finally found after you went away, after the salty taste of a million tears that spoke of eternity and one final sigh of acceptance. Your lessons were completed.

"The truth that transcends our deepest sorrows
is not the good that comes from the bad things
that happen, but the good that continues,
and even is revealed, despite them."

—Molly Fumia
Safe Passage, Words to Help the Grieving

Blessed Children
March 19, 1992

Kelly came into this world in a physical form that proved to be the catalyst for his incredible spiritual growth. When one is born with physical limitations, the spiritual aspect of that person's life will be amplified because everything in this world must be in balance. Just as a blind person's senses of touch, hearing and smell are heightened to offset the absence of sight, so God allows for other gifts to be embellished in a health-challenged child.

I have read many stories of physically challenged children. No matter what the disability, whether physical or mental, these children were infused with a light that penetrated the hearts of all whom they came in contact with. Even in the face of death, the children were fearless, even inspirational to those who cared for them. Their souls were so full of the love from which they came and to which they were returning.

I believe these children are given to this world as a pure gift of love. There is an energy attached to their souls that allows us all to experience life, as it is meant to be. No judgments, no false beliefs. Their lives and souls mirror only truth and that one huge truth is love.

These blessed children come to teach us a song we must all learn to sing. Through their physical or mental limitations they become our teachers and we, their students. They show us how fragile we are. They teach us to only attach to today; for yesterday is a recollection, and tomorrow is still a secret. So, in the process of learning to believe in unicorns, and being reminded to smell the rain, we shall become whole, we shall all be healed.

"It would seem that the cycle of life begins not
with birth, but rebirth. The newness of spring buds,
or babies, or facets of a relationship, comes not
from something that wasn't there before,
but from some old miracle of love that delights
in change. Death cannot jump the track of the
cycle and create a remnant from which newness
can grow. Death, like rebirth, must be on the way
around, over and over again."

—Molly Fumia
Safe Passage, Words to Help the Grieving

Blossoming
April 29, 1992

The day after the funeral, some dear friends brought a nectarine tree to our home to be planted in Kelly's memory (unaware that nectarines were Kelly's favorite fruit). Our friends helped us plant the tree and offered a special Native American prayer for its health and growth. One tiny pink blossom was open.

The next day I was in the kitchen writing, and a voice inside my head told me to go upstairs and look for pictures, which I did. In looking through photographs of Kelly, I found a small gift card with a flower on the front on which Kelly had written:

"Mom, now is the time to smell the flowers that you have grown and know that with a little dirt, sunshine and water that a blossom will come."

I began to cry. The single blossom on that tree was a gift—a gift from Kelly. The tree even had a little crooked trunk just as Kelly had a curved spine caused by scoliosis. The young tree grew at a funny little angle but was still strong.

On Valentine's Day a year later, the first buds on Kelly's Tree opened, a bouquet of three pink flowers. One for spirit, one for mind and one for body. The first year a nectarine tree is not supposed to bear fruit at all, but Kelly's Tree was heavily laden with tiny precious fruits.

We receive messages and gifts in many forms. They happen all around us, but we must be awake and aware in order to notice them. In the last few months, I have even been able to be grateful for Kelly's illness, for without it, we would not have known the closeness of the bond we shared.

It altered us. It made us both stronger and more compassionate individuals. And, ultimately, the intimacy that his illness and birth defect brought to our lives became an imprint on our souls, a connection between parent and child that, eventually, allowed me to conquer the devastation of saying goodbye, to conquer the pain of his death within my heart.

"The bird flies its way out of the egg. The egg is the world…
Who would be born must first destroy a world.
The bird flies to God…And it is always difficult to be born.
The chick does not find it easy to break out of the shell…
Nothing can be born without first dying."

—Hermann Hesse
Demian

The Teacher
May 4, 1992

This morning as I raised the shades in the kitchen windows, I noticed our mother cat and one of her kittens playing with something beneath a small shrub in our neighbor's back yard. At first, I thought it might be a field mouse.

Soon my gaze shifted to a bright red Cardinal, flitting from branch to branch of the small bush. I had been watching this bird for several months. He and his mate come daily to feast at the feeder in our back yard. Now he was dangerously close to the two cats—too close for his own safety. It was then I realized that the cats had one of his babies.

My heart ached for him. Helpless, he was not able to stop these animals from their instinctual act. I watched him as he looked on, only to see the lifeless body of *his* child. I knew in that moment that he and I shared a feeling—loss. I wished I could have rescued the baby bird from death, breathed life back into its tiny body and placed it safely back in the nest—to again feel the safety and warmth of its mother's feathered breast.

It is now evening and I find myself thinking about the baby bird's parents. I wonder how they are feeling. Surely they know that one is missing, that they witnessed their own loss today. And I wonder if the red bird will sing tomorrow and if he will have that little happy skip in his flight that I have found so delightful? Perhaps he will be silent. Somehow, in my heart,

I know that he will sing for me in the morning and continue to fly with that special, happy expression that is uniquely his.

As I continue to observe him, I will be searching for answers to these questions: What allows him to sing again so soon? Does he know a secret? Has God given him a greater wisdom than I possess?

My relationship with this winged one has now changed. He will continue to remind me of God's creation in my observances of him. I am aware now of a quiet strength that resides in him. He has become a teacher for me.

When I recall this lesson, I will be reminded of his loss and mine. I will be comforted by the knowledge that we will both sing again.

"What deep wounds ever closed without a scar?"

—Lord Byron (1788–1824)
British poet
Childe Harold's Pilgrimage

Familiar Melodies
April 8, 1993

Repetition seems to play some role in acceptance. If you listen to a song long enough, you memorize the words. If you tell the same story over and over again, it eventually will become an integral part of your life. And so it is with the loss of a child. If you are reminded again and again of the thought *Nothing you do will change this*, then it becomes like listening to a familiar melody. Something deep inside you begins to hear the words of the song, not just the melody.

In the beginning we hope that if we cry enough tears or scream enough at the injustice, God might know the depths of our pain and give our children back to us. But soon we learn that life will force us to move beyond this place. There does come a point of understanding—a knowing that the million tears we've cried, the pain we've felt were necessary. The greatest challenge then comes in confronting the reality of our children's absence from our lives—gone.

It's still hard to believe, even now.

"If thou should never see my face again,
Pray for my soul. More things are wrought with prayer
Than this world dreams of."

—Lord Alfred Tennyson (1809–1892)
British poet

A Prayer for Parents Who Have Lost a Child
August 1, 1993

Dear God, we offer this prayer.

We ask that you would be with us as we journey this path of sorrow. Please send a sign of hope, specific to each one who has lost a child. We ask that you would walk ahead of us on those days when we require guidance, and walk with us and hold our hand on those days when we stumble and need your companionship and greater understanding.

On the days when we see clearly, *the good days*, may we be ever mindful of the grace that has filled our lives—in the form of the child you gave to us as a gift.

On the days when we drink from the cup of tears, would you very gently remind us of the delight that once was ours. And on those *bad days*, please also help us to discern that these are the healing days. It is important for us to accept that we must weep great tears before we may begin to heal our broken hearts. If we could but look upon these tears as a salve for our wounds, we would welcome these days.

Help us, God, to be eternally grateful, even in the midst of our sorrow, for the love we have known because of our child. Help us to grow through this pain with the hope and love you provide through family and friends and your promises. Help us to know within our hearts that you have always loved our child as much as we do—and grant us peace in the days to come.

Amen.

"A cloud does not know why it moves in just such a direction and at such a speed. It feels an impulse…this is the place to go now. But the sky knows the reasons and the patterns behind all clouds, and you will know, too, when you lift yourself high enough to see beyond horizons."

—Richard Bach
Illusions, The Adventures of a Reluctant Messiah

Transcending the Pain
October 13, 1993

I cannot speak for the pain and loss experienced by others, for grief is unique to each individual. I may only tell you of my transcendence over loss. The act of transcendence is a significant and essential task.

My healing was composed of time, of full and honest acknowledgment of the pain I felt, and the final acceptance of an event in my life that no amount of prayer or bargaining with God would ever change. The final diagnosis: My only child, my son, was dead. I was to somehow integrate this pain and acceptance into a space that allowed both to exist, side by side, and healing would occur.

In the beginning, I had to become familiar with the pain in my heart. The final act: To bridge my heart to my mind and allow my mind to begin to acknowledge the truth of my loss; to fathom the depth of the emptiness I felt in my heart.

I cannot tell you exactly when or how the pain began to change or even subside for brief periods of time, but it did—just as one breath flowed into another, and with each beat of my heart. I can speak to you of a morning sunrise when I quietly waited for the colors to spread throughout the light in the eastern sky. On this day, my world was transformed.

As I watched the world awaken, I observed the clouds. The more I focused on the clouds and the colors, the more at peace I felt. The clouds were still, the sky unvarying in this cloud pattern. The clouds and the pastel morning light seemed pre-arranged to instill feelings of splendor and serenity.

I had once seen clouds such as these, painted on the sacred space of a cathedral ceiling. I was grateful for the solitude and for the moment in which I felt connected to God. For a moment, I felt as if a portal had opened, allowing me to penetrate the veil between heaven and earth. A deep and lasting peace washed over me.

I did not want the moment to end, but it did. The light expanded, the clouds changed places with each other, and the day began. The feeling of vast tranquility remained with me. I felt blessed to have shared the birth of the day and the beginning of my transcendence with my heart wide open, in the company of the spirit of my son and in the midst of angels.

"Mourning is like reentering the womb.
We find a dark place where we can weep unheeded
and become whole in our time. Emptiness
turns to hope in this safe refuge,
this comforting cavern echoing endings
and beginnings, slowly transformed again into
a passageway to our other, older life."

—Molly Fumia
Safe Passage, Words to Help the Grieving

Birthing Your Soul
January 5, 1994

What have I learned about the grief process? It took a long time, but I finally learned that I wasn't going to die from this profound pain and immense sorrow that lingered in the hallways of my house and heart. Because somewhere during this process of the real agony of separation and the long process of recovery, I made a decision to consciously examine the broken parts of my heart, one brittle shard at a time—to touch those places that were weary, worn and aching with memories. I peeled back the veil to my soul.

I knew my love for Kelly and his love for me was bigger than this pain and that this shared love would somehow sustain me through the darkness.

Remembering you …

In the beginning, I held your crumpled, plaid shirt to my face and wept. Eyes closed, I breathed you in—the lingering scent of your cologne remembered. I sat cross-legged on the tiger-oak floor of your bedroom with a life's worth of photographs of you encircling me, a black-and-white and colored paper shrine while I wept.

Your blond hair captured in your hairbrush was soft to my touch.

I traced the outline of your precise printing on a yellow pad with my fingertip, glancing at the names and addresses in your address book, knowing these friends of yours had gone on with their lives. I cried.

Once I slept with your big white teddy bear in the hope that some subtle whispered memory of you lingered there. But all that was left was the memory, and I wept some more at the vast immensity of your absence.

At birth, a baby must separate physically from its mother. The mother's body heaves and contracts in labor to push out this new life, causing the formation of two separate beings.

If a child dies, the sacred physical bond is severed forever between a parent and child. Inside the death of this child, a bereaved parent has been born. Hearts are heavy with grief. The pain is harsh and deep. Now the cycle of grieving begins. A parent must mourn the loss, grieve, find comfort, go deep, tell their story again and again. Finally, renewed by hope, love and grace, a parent will give birth to his or her own soul. It takes great courage to retrieve your soul and rebirth it following the death of a child. But it is possible and necessary.

"This eternal breath
like iris buds in moonlight
even as he dies."

—Rashani

Tethered to My Heart
November 20, 1994

If we never saw sunlight again would we miss it? Yes, but we would never forget its beauty or how it felt. We would remember the glorious gold-pink of sunrise, the ink-blue, claret sky of sunset, and the jeweled spectrum of a rainbow in a rain-washed sky.

I would remember the warmth of sunlight on my skin—like how my heart felt when you were born. That day the world was forever changed, and so was I.

They say that moonlight is a reflection of the sun's light. You were my sun. I was your moon. Your death eclipsed the light that illuminated my world, my soul. I long for moonlight again, but the memory of it has eased into that place where nothing is ever forgotten. In this sacred space, everything is eternal, floating free of the earth, but still tethered to my heart.

You have become my star—*my star child*—the light shining down on me from above, and forever and always shining within my heart.

"The impetus that makes you fly is our great human possession. Everyone has it. It is the feeling linked with the roots of power. But one soon becomes afraid of the feeling. That is why people shed their wings and prefer to walk and obey the law. But not you. *You* go on flying."

—Hermann Hesse
Demian

Flying Higher
March 17, 1995

My goddaughter, Joysa, wrote the quote that follows in a sympathy card. It is taken from the book *Jonathan Livingston Seagull* by Richard Bach. Reading these words always gave me a sense of peace, an inner knowing that perhaps Kelly's life was more complete than I could understand at the time of his death.

Just like Jonathan Livingston Seagull, my son had finished one school, and another was to begin. It was time for my child to fly, with understanding lighting his way and, in time, also illuminating mine.

I also felt comforted by the thought that there were others there in spirit for Kelly—just like the two gulls who appeared for Jonathan, who came to help him fly higher and take him back home.

> (The flock) came in the evening, then, and found Jonathan gliding peaceful and alone through his beloved sky. The two gulls that appeared at his wings were pure as starlight, and the glow from them was gentle and friendly in the high night air. But most lovely of all was the skill with which they flew, their wingtips moving a precise and constant inch from his own.
>
> "...And we fly now at the peak of the Great Mountain Wind" (Jonathan said). "Beyond a few hundred feet, I can lift this body no higher."
>
> "But you can, Jonathan, for you have learned. One school is finished, and the time has come for another to begin."

As it had shined across him all his life, so understanding lighted that moment for Jonathan Seagull. They were right. He *could* fly higher, and it was time to go home.

He gave one last look across the sky, across that magnificent silver land where he had learned so much.

"I'm ready," he said at last.

And Jonathan Livingston Seagull rose with the two star-bright gulls to disappear into a perfect dark sky.

"Stretch out your arms, my sister, so that
you may call the breath of Life deeply into you
and thus be made ready for the arrival of the child,
this *sacred star* from the deepest of space,
who even now soars across the heavens unto
your trembling arms…

Be not afraid to open your heart and mind
as well as your eyes, so that you shall
have full vision, for you are giving birth to
a glorious life."

—As revealed by Almitra through Jason Leen
The Death of the Prophet

The Death of the Prophet
May 10, 2001

The following excerpt is taken from the book *The Death of the Prophet*. The first time I read this, I felt a sense of peace wash over me, and each time I reread it, I feel the same. Jason Leen is correct: Even in the silence, the dance continues.

For even as you give birth unto your children, so shall they continue to be born anew unto the universe as each moment is born anew. And in that perpetual rebirth they are forever surrounded by love.

Verily, as they came dancing the dance of Life, so shall they continue to dance throughout the ages. Ay, for even as another has promised you, your life is without end.

Yet seek not to understand nor control the patterns of your children's dancing, nor become afraid when you can no longer hear the tune to which they step.

Rather would I have you relax your heart in peace, knowing that they dance but to the very music that has moved you—and that their movements have but altered themselves to better suit the nature of the dancer.

And become not consumed by sadness if your children's dancing should cease to be, for know beyond any doubt that the dance of Life continues on even though the dancer's steps are silent.

If you could but fathom this, you would be swept up into that very movement and soar beyond the boundaries of life and death.

For you are Light, created by Light from the essence of Light; and that which you create is Light.

Even as you give birth and the child moves from within your womb into the air of this world, it is but Light issuing from Light into Light.

"The truest measure of a life is not its length
but the fullness in which it is lived."
—Maria Housden
Hannah's Gift: Lessons from a Life Fully Lived

The Cries of Children
August 4, 2002

I am the one who cherishes your children, their cries, their laughter, the sweetness of their hugs or a blown kiss. My awareness has been expanded. I know the gift you hold in your arms, only because of the ones I have relinquished. I know how precious are these little lives.

It's August in Texas, and I'm seated at a table at Cheezy Jane's Restaurant with my husband. The lunch crowd is ordering hamburgers and malts, bean and cheese nachos, grilled chicken salads and soda fountain drinks. A miniature train glides soundlessly overhead, going around and around on a suspended ceiling track.

I saw you when you walked in, your little girl holding your hand, her blond ringlets peeking from beneath her petal-shaped sun hat. She looks about 3. Your two handsome sons, probably ages 6 and 8, with their buzzed summer haircuts, follow you to a table next to mine.

Your sons have your soft gray eyes. They call you Mommy and ask you a hundred questions, one after another. The oldest boy asks you how old he and his brother will be when you turn 50, when you turn 55, then 60.

You laugh and say, "That's a long time from now." The children busy themselves coloring and drawing with paper and crayons the waitress has brought them. Your little girl squats on the chair, her bare feet flat on the red vinyl seat, her tiny pink flip flops have silently tumbled to the floor. On her paper, she draws you a heart. You tell her to color it red. You smile tenderly at her, brush back a lock of hair from her face.

Shortly my husband and I get up to leave the restaurant, and I think about stopping briefly at your table to tell you how lovely your children are, remind you of how lucky and blessed you are. But I decide against it.

I think you know just how lucky and blessed you are. I see it in your eyes when you brush back your daughter's hair from her angelic face.

I am a wounded healer
I have walked a mile with pain
I have walked a mile with sorrow
I have walked a mile with shame

I was hiding in the darkness
In the silence of my cries
Till the sweet grace of my healer
Kissed my lonesome grief goodbye

Then he led me to my family
Those whose hearts could hold my pain
With that sweet grace they surround me
Never will I walk alone again.

Brother, Sister are you crying
Is your grief too much to bear
For I know the sweet grace of my healer
And your burdens I will share

Let me walk within your sorrow
Let me walk within your shame
For I am a wounded healer
Never will I walk alone again

Never will I walk alone again
Never will you walk alone again
My friend
My friend
My friend

From the song "Wounded Healer"
by Cary Cooper from *Gypsy Train*

Wounded Healer and Grace
October 15, 2002

I first heard Cary Cooper sing this song on October 6, 2002. Her clear, sweet voice filled the room and my heart with grace. I knew she knew. She was a wounded healer. This song was written from her soul, and she sings it just that way.

The lyrics to "Wounded Healer" say what my heart is feeling today. It has been many years now since Kelly died. I have felt his sweet presence during the process of creating *Star Child*, my *soul book,* as my friend Jeanette Schneider calls it. I hope Kelly is proud and honored. It's been a long night's journey but I have become a wounded healer along with Cary Cooper and the rest of humanity who have healed their pain from loss.

Another wounded healer and dear friend of mine, Peg Armstrong, is a retired bereavement specialist/therapist. She told me something once that I have never forgotten. She said, "When John F. Kennedy was killed. Jacqueline Kennedy, by her actions, taught Americans how to grieve: Don't cry. Don't show your pain. Be stoic."

Peg continued, "During the earthquake in Mexico, the relatives of the dead ripped off their shirts and screamed their grief to the heavens. They are practicing healthy grieving. They are expressing their pain. They will resolve their grief."

Later, Peg related another story of an American father whose son had committed suicide. The father told her, "You'll be proud of me—I haven't cried. I've been taking care of all the matters that need attending to. I've been keeping myself very busy." Peg was saddened to think that he believed she would be proud of him because he had not cried over the death of his son.

While working with Mother Theresa in India, Peg Armstrong deliberately held dying children. She described her feelings, "When the children died, I felt their bodies soften and their spirits leave. It was very peaceful; there was no pain."

Healing from the loss of a child is excruciating, but it's harder to stay in the pain, much harder. And it's not enough to just survive. Grief work is a spiritual journey governed by raw emotion. But, the journey through grief can also set you free.

A child's life is a gift. A child's death, sadly, is often part of that gift. But, it takes great courage to hold it, much less open it. But if you hold it long enough and do the grief work, your reward will be empowering compassion. Hearts that once were broken are now open, souls transformed. That's when grace happens. And when grace happens, things are never the same.

Although I am not Catholic, I am always struck by the mystical beauty of a Catholic funeral ceremony. The priest standing, arms outstretched, the sleeves of his vestment draping softly in the air. Then he speaks, "May the angels open wide the gates to Paradise." In that instant I know everything is okay. Our children are safe.

There are many paths from grief to grace. This has been my story. My healing took the course of talking about Kelly's death by attending the weekly support group, Forever Loved, and writing about my pain. I read many books written by parents who had lost children. I allowed myself to weep openly when the grief was too much to hold. Suppressed pain cannot heal.

I deliberately spent time in nature, taking walks or just sitting in the sun with eyes closed. In the spring, I planted flats of flowering plants. I nurtured the animals in our home, a mother cat and her four kittens.

As I became more healed, I tried to find other ways to *mother* by spending time with the young children of friends—four young girls, Jenny, Jessica, Lisa and Megan, who became the *goddaughters of my heart*. They took turns spending weekends at our home. They ravaged my closet, played dress-up with my clothes and always stayed up too late. I spoiled them, and they gave me their love and hugs. Their spirits and their laughter helped me to heal.

Today, these young girls are grown young women, but the love they gave me is still tucked in my heart. They let me love them and be their *other mother* just for a little while. And that's exactly what I needed at the time.

May you be guided to that which ministers to your soul. Heal your heart. Heal your world. Turn your pawn into a knight. Find your way home. Do whatever it takes to empty your heart of pain and allow Grace to envelop the sorrow.

May the tender brush of angels' wings dry your tears. May your heart be healed with these words that tumbled from my heart and mind like river-polished stones.

Just Under the Star
September 8, 2005

When I stumbled upon these words by French writer Antoine de Saint-Exupéry, I knew they would have to be a part of *Star Child*.

Writers are often told not to use someone else's words to finish their stories (because it might focus the reader's attention on someone else's writing instead of their own). I only wish I had written these words, for they do tell my story—the story in my heart, about a golden-haired boy and his mother who will always miss him and always wish he could come back.

For me, this is the loveliest and the saddest landscape in the world. It's the same landscape as the one on the preceding page, but I've drawn it one more time in order to be sure you see it clearly. It's here that the little prince appeared on Earth, then disappeared.

Look at this landscape carefully to be sure of recognizing it, if you should travel to Africa someday, in the desert. And if you happen to pass by here, I beg you not to hurry past. Wait a little, just under the star! Then if a child comes to you, if he laughs, if he has golden hair, if he doesn't answer your questions, you'll know who he is. If this should happen, be kind! Don't let me go on being sad: Send word immediately that he's come back...

—Antoine de Saint-Exupéry
The Little Prince

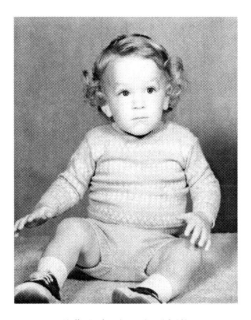

Kelly Hales (age 1—1968)

~

Dreams and Other Signs and Wonders

~

STEPHEN LEVINE

The following is Stephen Levine's experience of visiting with the mother of a young child dying of leukemia during his visit to Presbyterian Medical Center's Children's Hospital in New York City.

This is excerpted from his book Who Dies? An Investigation of Conscious Living and Conscious Dying.

An Extraordinary Contract

Another child I was asked to see was a 2½-year-old boy dying of leukemia. Besides being very weakened from the illness, he displayed several side effects of the treatment, including a severely fissured anus, blood clots in various places on his body, and a shunt to aid the induction of the chemotherapy he was undergoing. His body clearly reflected the degenerative state of his illness.

As I walked up to the metal crib in which Tony lay, he looked up at me and the two other people who accompanied me with eyes that seemed wide open to every possibility. His eyes stayed with each face for a few moments before moving on to share with the next. There was nothing cursory in his glance. He was completely present. Looking into his eyes was like looking into the night sky. He was so open to the moment, to death. He was so extraordinarily there for what was happening.

Although clearly Tony's body could hardly hold his life force, he did not withdraw, but instead moved toward this unknown spaciousness that he so willingly shared with all who came near. His acceptance of death was somehow transmitted to his mother, who later took me aside and asked me what she should do. She was confused because, although the most precious thing in her life was clearly moving beyond her touch, somehow in her heart there was an incredible okayness about it. She feared there was something the matter with her. Her husband, a career military man, insisted that his boy was not going to die. He found it very difficult to visit, to see his son so close to death, to experience the peace in that room.

Tony's mother and I spent some time together, sitting in another room, talking about how it was for her, feeling such openness and yet such confusion. She spoke of a warmness in the sharing with her son. And she said that somehow she could understand, could feel—not intellectually, but in her heart of hearts—that there was a contract between her and Tony that was bringing each to a fulfillment for which they had been born, but she said she couldn't imagine how this was so.

And I said:

"Well, can you imagine, can you just fantasize for a moment that there are these two unborn beings, floating between births, with love and great concern for each other's well-being? One of these beings turns to the other and says, 'You know, there's so much to be learned in a lifetime, I wonder if we couldn't help each other. Imagine if one of us were born a woman and, at 31, had this beautiful, incredible shining child. Every mother's dream of angelic perfection and loving-kindness. Then, let's say after sharing two years of life, the child is found to have some serious illness that evicts him from the body. And these two beings are forced to share the loss of this powerful contact. They share it in love, not holding on to the body, but remaining in each other's heart to complete the experience.'

These two beings, between births, sit down and say, 'Well, that sounds fruitful. Let's do it. One of us can be the 2-year-old and die surrounded by love, and the other can be the mother, so confronted with all that has kept her separate that she completely surrenders her knowing and just remains in her heart, in the very essence of the contact she has with her son, as she watches his body deteriorate beyond her control.' And it takes her to the direct experience of what's real. Her heart opens more fully than ever before.

So, one being turns to the other and says, 'Well, I'll be the mother.'

'No, no,' says the other, 'You did that another time. I'll be the mother.'

'No, no, I'll be the little boy.'

'No, no.'

And so they flip for it. And one comes in and thirty years later the other one comes through, and they play it out."

Tony's mother said that somehow she could feel the truth of this possibility. Her body could shake with tears at the loss of her son and yet her heart could remain open to whatever possibility might arise. And so, they made their choice and now they find themselves playing out the end game of this extraordinary contract to bring each other to deeper awareness and compassion.

A few weeks later, Tony left his body and his mother told me that somehow she knew beyond reason, beyond anything that anyone could tell her, that it was all right for him to do so. The work they had to do was completed with grace and love with which it may originally have been intended. After the death, Tony's father was grieving greatly, with much anger and guilt and confusion; he felt that he could never resolve it in the way his wife had.

Then a few days later, at the funeral, he had a most unexpected experience. For a moment his eyes shone with understanding and he turned to his wife and said, "I guess I know what you mean. Somehow I know it's all right for Tony to have died. I know he is okay and doing exactly what he needs to do for himself."

The growth and closeness that they shared was unparalleled by any other moment in their lives. And though they grieved the loss of their son, they also experienced great joy and fullness. An opening into the oneness that death cannot shatter, that cannot be separated, that does not depend upon a body for the communication of love and the sharing of the very essence that we are.

NANCY LEWIS WASKOW

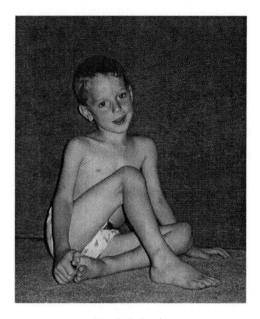

Heath A. Lewis

Nancy Lewis Waskow's son, Heath, died at the age of 4½ when he was hit by a car. Nancy was one of the extraordinary mothers I met in the Forever Loved support group. This is from her journal.

Finding Forgiveness

On April 14, 1991, I was trying to get a home alarm system to shut off when I turned around and saw that my 4½-year-old son, Heath, had crossed the street to play at a school playground. My son was on the other side of the street and my nephew, Jeremy, was on my side. The boys were talking and it looked like Jeremy would cross over also. I screamed, "Jeremy, stop!" at which time he did, and he turned to look at me. My son also turned to look at me, and his eyes popped open, knowing I was going to be angry at him, and he ran back to me suddenly. I didn't have time to scream again; it all happened in the matter of one-two seconds. My son was hit by a car and killed.

I don't know how I lived through that scene, or the ensuing long-suffering and grief. I know that if it had been my decision, I would not have lived. I would have gladly chosen not to, even though I still had two daughters to care for. I didn't feel like I could take care of them, since I had lost one child while in my care. I was haunted by demons following me around, in the dark, while I was alone.

I asked the children's babysitter if she would move in with us and help me take care of the girls since I no longer trusted myself; and I needed someone to be with me until I fell asleep at night since I was so afraid. Every morning for two weeks, I would go to speak with the church counselor, begging, crying, questioning; he finally told me I needed to see a real counselor. I frightened him, and he didn't know how to help me. What do you say to a mother who has just lost a child? Every day for one year I fought the urge to drop to my knees in front of a passing car, so that I may feel what he felt, because I deserved it.

I found a support group of parents who had lost children. They met weekly, and they saved my life. I felt I was a bad person and God took my son from me to teach me a lesson. In this group I met many good, honorable Christian families, and they, too, had lost a child. I realized, finally, that God didn't take my son from me, choices did that, and God was there to pull me through it, if I would allow it. I realized that even though I thought I was praying every day, almost all day, I was actually praying to my son, not to God.

I learned about faith, hope and prayer. I learned that good people have to die so the world will know about compassion, caring and forgiving. So many people grew from my son's death, and so did I. I think ahead for consequences more than I used to.

Spontaneous decisions usually lead to momentary happiness, not long-term happiness. Life should be lived to its fullest each day so no one should ever give up searching for possibilities or opportunities. We are responsible for our own actions and happiness, and the only person you can change is yourself.

Just over a year after my son's death, when I began praying to God for guidance and support, as well as thanking him for the precious years he gave me with my son, I received a dream to help me in my grief. There is no doubt in my mind that God gave me this dream.

I dreamed that I was awakened by a light at the foot of my bed. I could hear a powerful surge of electricity as this light drew me to it. Although no words were spoken out loud, I remember my heart was screaming in pain, it was constricted so tightly, and my throat was sore with unshed tears. Inside the light was my son. I cried out my longing, my pain, questioning him on his suffering and well-being, begging for forgiveness. The light engulfed me, and I was holding my son again, and he was holding me tightly and kissing me.

Suddenly my excruciating pain was replaced with rainbows of happiness, and overwhelming love and peace. I felt this happiness and well-being and his love for me. I felt forgiveness. Slowly, the light left my body and the room, and I slowly lay back down and fell into immediate sleep. When I awoke the next morning, I remembered the dream as I awakened. I knew he had been there. I knew it had happened.

Just as my son was chosen to help teach the world about compassion, caring, loving and forgiveness, I was chosen to have this dream and to speak of my faith. Life is filled with so many trials for each of us, and no matter how difficult those trials may be, just remember to believe in God to lead you through it.

Although I still make mistakes in my life, even when I believe I practiced the correct decision-making process, I know God knows that I tried. He forgives me for my mistakes, as he knows I am trying to be the best that I can be.

MARIANNE WOFFORD

Jason Gresham Wofford

Marianne and John Wofford's son and only child, Jason, died at the age of 10 from a gun accident. What follows are some premonitions and dreams Marianne shared with me. Marianne was one of the inspiring mothers I met in the Forever Loved support group.

Give Him a Kiss

I gave birth to Jason at 5:30 in the morning. Over the years, as Jason grew older, he developed a habit of waking at around this same time each morning, bringing his pillow and a palette and laying on the floor next to our bed. Just months before he died, it was a spring morning when I awoke at 5:30 a.m. to see Jason laying on his palette beside our bed. A voice in my head said, *Kiss him, give him a kiss. Because you may not have that many more times to kiss him.* So I did. He looked so beautiful and peaceful.

Two months after Jason died, I was in excruciating pain and grief and made the decision to visit a minister of ours, whom Jason had been very close to. Recently the minister had been transferred from an Episcopal church in Cuero, Texas, where we lived, to a church in Seguin, Texas.

When I arrived at the church, the minister greeted me. We talked for a while and then he made a suggestion that I visit the little church that had originally been built in the 1890s. It was located directly behind the more recently constructed large church. The minister suggested I might enjoy the architecture. Inside the small church, I knelt down at the altar and immediately began to cry. I started saying The Lord's Prayer. Suddenly, all the pain was gone, and I had the most wonderful feeling of peacefulness and love.

This is what Jason has, I thought. I would be a very selfish mother to ask him to leave that. That thought has stayed with me forever.

Later when I would have *visits* from Jason, I would feel a touch on my arm or a touch to my face. I would always know it was him because I felt that wonderful love and peacefulness that he would bring and that I know I can look forward to having in life after death.

When the Tennis Shoes Touch the Floor

When Jason was 2 years old, he was sitting on my lap, very content, his little tennis shoes touching the side of the wicker rocking chair. I was stroking his hair and telling him what pretty hair he had, loving him and kissing him when the thought came into my head, *When the tennis shoes touch the floor, he will be gone.*

And I thought, *No.*

When he was 10 years old, Jason and I were sitting in the same position in the rocking chair. Again I'm touching his hair and telling him what beautiful hair he has when I recall that moment when he was 2 years old and that voice in my head. *When the tennis shoes touch the floor, he will be gone.*

I looked down at Jason's feet and his tennis shoes *were* touching the floor. I acknowledged the memory of when he was 2 years old, but again I refused to accept it. Two weeks later, Jason died.

In retrospect, I believe it was said to me twice. Once to tell me I would have more time with him, the second time to say, *Are you listening?"*

Leaving Soon

From the time Jason was 9 years old, I now believe, he knew on some level that he was going to die. He would hug and kiss me at every opportunity and tell me I was the greatest mother in the world (a gift for me to cherish later).

Jason was an extraordinarily sensitive, kind and compassionate child. He expressed unconditional love to everyone, was a thoughtful and motivating child. Everyone loved him. In May of the year he turned 10, my husband's father died that same month. In August of that year, Jason was sitting at the island in the kitchen, crying.

"Jason, what is it?" I asked.

He just shook his head.

"Are you upset about grandpa? Do you want to go to the cemetery?" I asked. He didn't respond. I wanted to make sure he had an opportunity to express his feelings so I drove him to the cemetery.

At the cemetery, Jason's grandpa and grandma are buried side by side. Their plot is surrounded by a concrete border. Jason never acknowledged his grandpa's grave but instead stood in an area below the grave. There he stood and looked down at the ground and cried big tears. Finally, Jason and I sat down on a nearby curb, and we talked about death. I told him that we all come to this earth to live, we get old and we die. We talked at length about death and dying.

As I said, I don't believe Jason consciously knew he was going to die. I believe this incident happened to help prepare me—to let me know that he would be leaving soon. On some level, we both knew he was going to die—we just didn't know why or how. In October of that year, Jason *did* die. The gravesite over which he stood and cried those big tears turned out, ultimately, to be his burial place. The choice of that location was not intentional on our part.

Laid Down by Angels

In our old house, we had a storeroom off the carport. It was a long narrow room, probably 8 by 15 feet, and contained a freezer and refrigerator. It was also where my husband stored his guns, propped up against a wall. The room was usually kept locked.

Two months before he died, I found Jason standing in the storeroom staring out the window looking at the sky. He stood there, arms straight down at his side, staring outside, mesmerized, as if he were in some sort of trance. Jason never moved or acknowledged my presence as I entered the storeroom. He never turned his head or seemed to notice I was there.

"What you are doing in here?" I asked.

"I don't know," he said, never turning his head or moving.

"Come on out. You don't need to be in here."

At that, Jason finally turned and followed me out of the storeroom.

The day Jason died, I found him lying on his back in the storeroom, as if he'd been laid down by angels. The light was dim, but I could see that he was wearing a T-shirt, shorts and tennis shoes. I could see his face. When I touched his forehead, it moved as if it were made of rubber. I knew immediately he was dead.

I was led back out of the room as if I were being pulled back by a presence. I ran through the house screaming, then outside, screaming. That day there were some people, men and one woman, trimming trees in our yard. They heard my screams and came running toward me. Hurriedly, we all went to the storeroom. One man went in. He screamed, then ran out.

The woman and I went inside the house. I sat down in the wicker rocking chair and recited phone numbers for the funeral home, the police, and a number where my husband, John, could be reached. The woman made the phone calls.

It was in that moment, when I sat in the same wicker rocking chair, that I knew that Jason was really dead. The thought, *I knew this was going to happen* filled my mind.

The day I found Jason's body in the storeroom, I saw nothing that would remain in my mind to haunt me—no image of my son that would pain me, unlike the man who also went inside.

Before Jason's death, I didn't believe in life after death. My son's death gave me three gifts:

To know, without a doubt, that there is a life after death;

To know that Jason has the peacefulness and love that I experience each and every time he visits me;

and To know there is positively a God who has worked in my life before Jason's death and continues to do so after his death.

LINDA SVOBODA

Michael Benishek

Linda Svoboda's son, Mike, was murdered at the age of 24 when he was attempting to help a transient. The writings that follow are from her journals—she was one of the insightful mothers I met in the Forever Loved support group.

Dimes From Heaven

Mike Benishek—*a handsome, vibrant, free-willed beautiful soul, whose life ended tragically when he was murdered by a drifter*
Linda Svoboda—*Mike's mom*
Sylvia May—*a dear friend of both Mike and Linda. Sylvia was born and raised in Agua Caliente, Mexico. She has a very open mind, believes she has dreams with meanings and is very open to the possibility of loved ones being able to communicate from the other side. Mike would always say "Mama is my mama, but Sylvia is my mentor."*

It all started about three months after Mike died. I was doing everything I could do just to hang on, but Sylvia was having an even harder time. We always walked together in the evenings, but I had stopped it. I just didn't have the emotional strength to hold Sylvia up anymore.

A friend of ours decided to have us all over for supper one Saturday night just to get our minds off Mike for a little while. I was dreading being with Sylvia—every time she saw me she would start crying. However, this night she was calm and seemed excited. After awhile when we were alone together, she said, "Guess what? Mike came to see me."

It took me a couple of seconds to realize that she meant he had come to her in a dream. She had awakened one morning and drifted back to sleep when she heard footsteps on her saltillo tile floor. She said she knew it was Mike because it sounded like he was dragging his foot. Mike had one foot smaller than the other, and when he wore a pair of loafers, one would slip and click against the floor. I had thought of that just that same morning when my own shoe happened to slip from my foot and clicked against the tile floor. I had kept doing it because it sounded so good, reminding me of Mike's walk.

Sylvia said she sat up in bed and found Mike standing by her bed. She said she fussed at him because it took so long for him to come and see her. The main gist of the conversation was that he couldn't stay long. He told her that everything was wonderful. He was so happy but he had to get back. He said it was a very important day; he was going to be *beamed.*

Sylvia asked him what that meant. He told her he didn't know, but he knew he couldn't be late. From then on, Sylvia had peace; she knew Mike was all right and would come again to visit her.

A couple of months later, Sylvia told me Mike had come to see her again in a dream, reappearing in the very same way: She heard Mike walk into her room just as he had done before. Again, she fussed at him for taking so long to come back to see her.

He told her he had been so busy that he hadn't had time. He also told her the day that he had to get back because he was going to be *beamed* was the day he had become an angel.

Sylvia said, "You, an angel? Mike, don't give me that."

"I've always been an angel, Sylvia—but now I'm a real one," he said, laughing.

Sylvia said she wanted proof. Mike put his hand in his pocket and pulled out a shiny dime and handed it to her. She asked him what that meant and he told her that she would find out. The next day Sylvia found a dime in the washing machine, which excited her very much. I didn't really think too much about this until I started finding dimes myself.

One night my 2½-year-old grandson was spending the night with us. At 11:30 p.m. he decided he wasn't going to sleep with his daddy, and he wanted to sleep in my bedroom with me and my husband. I made him a bed on the floor. I looped a comforter and a blanket over in thirds for softness and wrapped a sheet around both of them. The next day I started folding up the bedding and found a dime between the blanket and the quilt. This moment was very special to me. It had been just a month before when my grandson, Cody, had told me that he could see Mike standing behind me.

Over the years I have found so many dimes that I have quit counting them. I always find them in very unusual places. Every time I tell my dime story to someone, they, too, will start finding dimes—especially my family. One time my mother was on her hands and knees in the backyard pulling weeds and found a dime in the grass.

One of my fears after Mike died was that he would be forgotten. Now I have people who never had the opportunity to meet Mike get so excited when they find a dime, especially when something unfortunate has happened to them, they believe they have their own personal guardian angel.

Shortly before Mike was killed, he was talking with his co-worker about death and losing loved ones. Mike said that he hoped he would die before his mama because it would kill him to have to bury her. His friend asked him, "What about your poor mama who would have to bury you?" He told her he knew his death would make his mama extremely sad, but that she was stronger than he was and could better survive.

"Besides," he said, "I know I won't live to be an old man, but will die young."

His co-worker told him he was full of it.

Mike turned around. Peeking over his glasses, he said, "I may die young, but I will be back."

He kept his word.

He's Standing Right Behind You

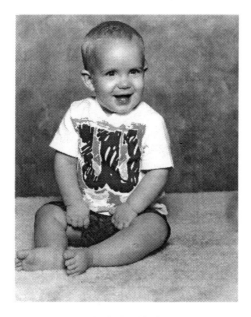

Cody Benishek

Besides my son, Mike, I also have two other sons, Bob and Bill. I also have two grandchildren, Megan, who was 8 at the time of Mike's death and Cody who was not quite 2½. Both attended the funeral services for Mike.

Megan was really sad. Cody seemed to have cared less. I don't know that he actually viewed Mike's body. I don't think so, but either way death doesn't seem to mean a lot to a 2½-year-old.

Months following Mike's death, my older son, Bob, who was working in Houston at the time, would come home every other weekend and bring Cody with him. Right from the very start, Cody started talking about Uncle Mike, which I thought was a little strange because Cody hadn't spent much time with Mike. My sons lived in different cities and maybe would only get together about twice a year. Two weeks after Mike's death, Cody came in with a new haircut.

I told him, "Oh Cody, I like your new hair cut."

He ran his hand through his hair like a normal little boy messing it all up and then said, "Uncle Mike cut my hair."

I told him, "No, honey, I don't think Uncle Mike cut your hair."

He argued back, "Yes him did, him cut my hair!"

I just chalked it up to the fact that Mike had given him his first hair cut and had attempted to cut it one other time. I thought maybe Cody was confused and thought the barber who cut his hair resembled Mike.

My son, Bob, was divorced from Cody's mother. On Mother's Day weekend, nearly four months after Mike's death, Bob had made his usual Houston to Corpus Christi trip to pick up Cody, and then drove on to our home, at the time in Pleasanton. We ate supper and then Cody went next door to play with one of the neighbor's children. Bob sat at the breakfast bar that wrapped about the kitchen area while I cleaned up the kitchen.

He said to me, "You know, Mom, Cody has been doing something very strange. Ever since Mike died—every weekend we come here—as we drive past the cemetery Cody always talks about Mike."

Keep in mind, this isn't the cemetery where Mike was buried—he was buried in Floresville, Texas, 25 miles away.

"Maybe it's because it was the last place he can associate with Mike," I suggested.

"I don't know, it's just very strange," Bob said. "Nearly every time he'll be playing with something and look up just in time for the cemetery and say, 'There's where Uncle Mike is.' Tonight it happened again. We drove by the cemetery and Cody looked up and said, 'There's Uncle Mike again.' I finally acknowledged him for the first time and told him 'Yes, Cody, Uncle Mike is there, but he's sleeping.' Cody looked at me and said, 'Uncle Mike's not sleeping. He's awake.'"

Bob said he kind of teased him by asking him if he could see Uncle Mike—what was he doing?

Cody responded by saying, "Oh nufin'—just flyin' around."

Bob said, "You know, Mom, we as adults, if we think of spirits or ghosts we might think they could fly or float around, but how would a 2½-year-old know that?"

I agreed it was a little strange but just brushed it off.

A few minutes later, Cody came bounding into the kitchen asking if I had any pudding for him. I told him I did and to crawl up at the breakfast bar and sit by his daddy, and I would get him a pudding cup. (You have to know through the whole story that I am about to tell you, the most important thing to Cody was that he get to hold his pudding cup and feed himself.)

I agreed but leaned across the inside of the breakfast bar with wash cloth in hand to catch drips. As Cody ate his pudding, Bob asked me if I had heard from the district attorney's office. I had and we talked a little bit about it, and the conversation just went basically dead.

I could tell Bob was deep in thought and then he said, "You know what Cody is saying about Mike is really starting to spook me, and you know I don't spook easily."

"Oh you mean that he says he can see Mike?"

Cody looked up at me and said, "I can, I can see Uncle Mike."

"Oh, you can?"

"Yep."

"Well, Cody," I said jokingly, "If you can see your Uncle Mike, the next time you see him would you please tell him Meme (me) loves him."

Cody glanced up from his pudding and looked straight in my eyes. "You tell him, he's standin' right 'hind you."

I turned around suddenly. Because of the look on Cody's face, I truly believed that I would see something there, but, of course, saw nothing.

"Cody, I don't see anything."

"Turn around. He's standin' right 'hind you in the kitchen."

Again I turned around. Again I saw nothing.

"Cody, I still don't see anything."

Cody didn't look up this time—remember, the most important thing to him was that I didn't get too close to the pudding he was attempting to eat. He just shrugged his shoulders and said very casually, "He's standin' right 'hind you in the kitchen."

By this time Bob and I were totally speechless and more than a little shocked. Then I asked Cody a question that I really don't know where it came from.

"Cody, is your Uncle Mike happy?"

Cody stopped stirring his pudding, looked over my right shoulder and said, "Yep, he smilin'." And without missing a lick went right back to his pudding, like it was no big deal.

There are no words to describe what that weekend has done for me.

MITCH CARMODY

Kelly Carmody

This poem, from the book *Letters To My Son: A Journey Through Grief* by Mitch Carmody, reflects the belief that while we live in one state of existence and our loved one who has died in another, through undying love, faith and desire we can meet in that shadowy place where our worlds connect. The book has now reached the bereaved in almost every state and seven other countries.

From the book's success, Mitch travels the country lecturing on the grief process and how to survive the loss of a loved one. He has dedicated his life to helping those individuals and families who are trying to navigate the uncharted territory of death, dying and the bereavement process.

To purchase a signed copy of *Letters to My Son: A Journey Through Grief:* *www.heartlightstudios.net*

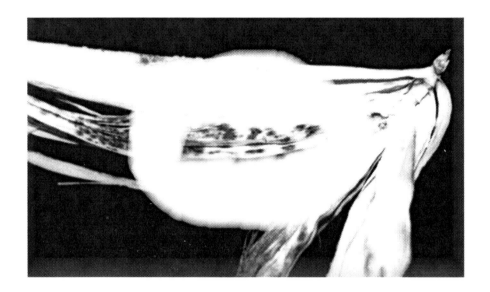

The Three Cornstalks

In December of last year
my young son passed away
I wanted proof that he survived
so I would talk, when I did pray.

I asked him for a sign
that would grow in our yard this spring
not a timely rainbow
or a bird on a wing.

I requested a living indication
that Kelly would manifest
growing from God's green earth
a portent at my request.

That summer we had a drought
the ground as dry as bone

but yet from the parched & dried up lawn
three plants grew all alone.

Three corn stalks grew
where none had grown before
no seeds were ever planted
amongst the weeds galore.

These three corn stalks formed a triangle
its terminus pointing southwest
toward the land of Kelly's healing
and the miracle that we knew best

Later in the summer
the northwest corn stalk withered and bent
like the loss of Kelly's childhood
before his life was spent.

A few weeks later
the northeast corn stalk died
just as Kelly's physical body had
where his soul had chosen to reside.

The last corn stalk survived
and bore fruit for all to see
a sacred symbol of Mexico
are the corn stalks three.

This year on the first of December
a mourning dove sat at our door
beseeching us to watch her
for the message that she bore.

This bird captivated us
as she hopped across the lawn
then flew over the lone corn stalk
and in a moment…was gone.

I trudged through the snowy yard
anticipation thick in the air
my intuitive senses reeling
in hopes of what could be there.

I examined the dried and withered stalk
for a message it might contain
and near the bottom nearly covered with snow
one last ear did remain.

I plucked this last and lonely ear
pulling its yellowed husk slowly back
within I found a tiny cob
with mold of green and black

This putrefaction of the cob
imprinted a word that could be read
stained clearly on the yellow husk
the word "DAD" was all it said.

~

Healing Words and Other Heart Things

~

BRENDA RABALAIS

Lee Rabalais

Brenda Rabalais, PhD, LMFT, is the president of Lee's Place, a nonprofit grief and loss counseling center she founded in Florida in 2000 in the memory of her son, Lee Rabalais, who died at the age of 14 of bone cancer.

It is the mission of Lee's Place to provide counseling and educational services to those who are adjusting to a loss. Some of these losses include divorce, abandonment (foster care, adoptees, etc.), death, imprisonment and other life transitions. Lee's Place, 216 Lake Ella Drive, Tallahassee, FL 32303; www.leesplace.org

The Conundrum of Grief

I'm always amazed at how contradictory I feel when I read other people's stories of experiences of loss. On the one hand, I'm impressed at how eloquent the writings can be—descriptive, shocking, similar or different from my own experiences with death, tender, terrible or transformative. On the other hand, I'm always amazed at how words never really touch the level of grief in my heart. But neither does music, or dancing, or anger, or art. But then that is the conundrum with grief, isn't it?

Grief is something that cannot find full expression in this world. So what do we do with it? We do what humans can do: we write, we paint, we sing, we dance. All in the hopes of somehow expressing on the outside what we know on the inside. And the wheel turns.

SHELLY WAGNER

Your Questions

I'll tell you;
I'll be bold.
You cannot know what this is like.
I don't want you to know
firsthand. But do not dare surmise
or worse, pass judgment–
you'll hear a different poem from me.
Not the poem that tries
with constricted throat
to speak the unspeakable,
recapture in foolish, shallow syllables
the trauma of loss
so you might
know for a moment
grief that gives life,
transcends,
blesses with wisdom.
It's my choice to share these lessons.
It's your choice to not listen
if you cannot bear
what I also thought
I could not survive.
I will understand
and wait
until you need this lesson
like a lifeline
when you are drowning.

You will die, too, you know.
There's nothing I can do about it
but have you drown in my poem
for only a moment,
then come gulping to the surface
looking into my eyes
smiling because you are not dead
but happier than you were before
to shake the water off your head,
go home and kiss your children,
tuck them in bed,
sleep yourself unsettled
but wake somehow refreshed.
So I will keep telling my story,
what I know to be true.

I am different.
I felt it right away.
I wanted to die to be
with Andrew.
Others knew;
some forced themselves to touch me
as though my flesh *had* fallen away,
leaving my skull
to remind everyone of death.
It has taken me years
to recognize my face in the mirror,
to know who I am,
but I tell you
my face shines like Moses' face
and I refuse to hide it anymore,

cover it with makeup
or put on a smile
to make it easier for you.
Do not avoid my eyes.
Do not walk away from me.
I am a mother.
Come close, sit down
and listen.

We'll begin with your questions.
Ask me, for example,
why you never received a thank-you note
for flowers, food
or charity contributions
because I need to tell you.
After the funeral, I threw away
the funeral home's inadequate
thank-you notes given to me in a box.
I intended to write all of you,
but years went by,
and I never thanked you
for salvation in flowers,
nourishment of fried chicken,
poetry in "Given in memory of...."
One day I hope to see
the Jerusalem pine a friend planted in Israel,
Andrew's oak pew in a new chapel by the beach,
a music room full of children singing
where his memorial plaque proclaims:
"Make a joyful noise."
When my knees buckled,

I fell backward
onto your gifts like pillows
and like a person convalescing
propped them around me.
Now that I am better I can
write a long note to say thank you
and I love you
and I'm sorry it all happened.

For words of comfort even now,
you might say and some did say,
"You still have another son."
Now I ask you,
"Do you hear
your logic?
When your mother died
did your living father make it easier?"
What saved you, you ask?
Unconditional love.
I was lucky with Andrew.
We were happy.
Nothing left undone.
Our last moments together were filled
with laughter. Pushing him in his tire swing
by the river,
he was curled inside the circle
like a baby in the womb,
giggling
because he knew at random
I would catch him,
hold him close to my heart,

unwilling to let go,
and cover his face with kisses.
Fill your relationships
with all the photos in your mind
until they are so good
you will be afraid of losing them, and you will.
But that will not kill you,
you'll survive and live on.
It's regret that destroys you,
anything left undone.
You see I tell you
what you already know.
Don't shake your head
and dismiss this because it is simple.

Let's pretend you have climbed
a dangerous mountain,
reached the summit to see
the wise old woman who lives on the peak.
Your bruised knuckles knock on her door.
It opens. She's standing there–
you can't believe it–
wearing shorts,
her hair pulled back in a rubber band.
You've come all this way,
it's not what you expected
and worse yet
she goes to her desk,
gives you a paper,

one of hundreds, all typed,
"Live each day as though it were your last."

You see our problem,
you already have this at home
in a needlework picture.
Because it is nothing new
you may turn away,
but I won't worry about you.
You are a climber,
an asker of questions
with answers
cross-stitched on your walls at home,
hung in old frames on a nail,
hiding a flaw in the plaster.

I'll ask the next question of you
because you may not think to wonder,
"Is there anything you would have done differently?"
Yes, I'd bring his body home,
put his blue casket in my living room,
group all the flowers around him.
Imagine all the flowers.
Think of two more days
for me to look at my child,
discover the bruise
on his forehead that wasn't there
when we were playing.
I learned of his injury
weeks later
when the funeral director told me,

"He was so beautiful.
We did nothing but cover the blow."
For two more days
I could have spoken to my child face to face
before forced to speak
only to darkness or you.
There were not enough chances
to touch him,
put my cheek next to his.
I wouldn't have been afraid
of my child's body;
but I left him at the funeral home
in the corner room
on the second floor
and visited whenever I could
because I did not want to scare you.

Next time will be different.
I'll put my loved one in the house
like my mother's family used to do,
and we'll all gather around
like sitting by a fire.
At the cemetery, like a rabbi
I'll take the shovel
and heap the dirt back in the hole,
do the raking and sodding myself.

Let me tell you.
You would not know to ask
about the day they set his tombstone.
I watched them stand the small granite cross

in a footing of wet cement.
When the workers left,
I touched the stone
carved with his name in full
because that's the way he said it,
written in all capitals
because that's the way he wrote it:
ANDREW CAMERON MINTON.
I broke a branch
so I could write to my child
in the margin of wet cement,
"I love you. I miss you.
Thank God I will see you again."
You see I have learned
chances don't come again.
I listen when they say,
"Opportunity is brief.
Remember cement gets hard.
Yesterday is set concrete
unable to record your words."

Shall we go on? I have seven years to tell you.
I read the next question in your eyes:
"How have you managed to go on?"
You'll hate my answer:
more needlework,
perhaps a needlepoint pillow?
Let me paint
the canvas for you.
Now go home with your fists
full of rainbows of wool,

thread the needle yourself,
strain to see
through your tears,
pull each thread through the holes,
in and out like a pulse.
Nail your finished canvas on a frame,
stretch it square,
bind it with cord
braided of your hair.
Put it on your sofa, show it to your friends,
teach them *One Day At a Time.*

No more questions, but you are concerned.
You suggest I get out and get some exercise.
Exercise!? Exercise!?
Grief is isometric.
Are you looking at my face?
I have the face of a sprinter.
I grimace and strain
like the runners I saw
in the New York marathon.
Those toward the end were suffering,
dying, though more alive than most of us
cheering for people we didn't know,
"Don't give up! Keep going!"
Some were passing them water.
The runners ran on, some fell skinning their knees.
If you pass me a cup of water
you will see
what I see up the road—
a rugged uphill course I'm determined to finish.

I'll make it
if I pace myself,
forgive myself when I fall,
and stop long enough to accept the water you offer.

Communion

On the first anniversary of your death,
I went to the kitchen,
set the table with your Superman place mat
and pulled up your chair.
I made a peanut butter and jelly sandwich,
removed the crust as always
for a special occasion.
I cut it into quarters
and arranged the triangles
on your red plate.
I poured milk in your blue plastic
Crayola crayon mug,
put on its pointed top
with the hole in the tip for a straw.
I had no straws.
I don't buy them anymore.
Sitting next to your place,
I apologized for no straw.
I apologized for your death.
I apologized for not being there.
When I finished,
I wiped my eyes with your napkin,
gave thanks,
ate the bread and drank the milk.

The Dinner Party

The sun squints curiously
behind eyelids of clouds
to watch me string the dogwood
with white Christmas lights.
I swim through the spider webs
hanging off each limb.
The webbed shroud has covered
the tree all summer,
its delicate silver cords
grasp the white roses
that weep and fall
over the stone wall.
The tide comes in
to see my foolishness,
asks with its chin
on the bulkhead,
"Christmas lights in August?"
Company is coming for dinner.
We will eat outside
under the tree,
clink our glasses
like a bell choir.
The cicadas will accompany us
with shrill rattles
as they escape
the brittle molds of themselves,
leaving exact likenesses
on the trunk of the tree.

I will ask my young guests
about their babies and toddlers.
They will tell me they never knew
they could love so much
and know so little.
I'll tell them
to have at least four children
and quote my grandmother
who would say,
"You are eating your white bread and butter."
It will be Christmas
under the illuminated tree.
They will give me gifts
of beautifully wrapped stories
containing small children,
huge hearts,
fragile futures.
When they leave,
I will kiss each one
in case I never see them again.
I'll leave the lights on all night.
The next day, I will clear the table
and the spider webs
that return during the night.
I'll collect the empty cicada shells,
line them up on the table where we dined—
a little cicada parade—
the way my children did when they were small

and lived here. One story
I keep for myself.

The Pearl

Never saying goodbye,
I return over and over
to sit on the dirt mattress
covered with the bright green grass blanket
made from seed sewn by your grandfather.
Unlike the mother and child we once were,
you have gone without my permission,
not holding my hand,
through a door I cannot open.
At the grave,
you are now the wiser one
but death will not let you
give me answers.
And would I believe you if you said,
"The pain that has come between us
will someday be our pearl?"

EDWIN ROMOND

Edwin Romond is a poet who was a public school educator for 32 years before retiring in 2003. His book of poetry, Dream Teaching, *is available from Grayson Books. Contact Edwin Romond at* <u>*www.edwinromond.com*</u>

Last Touch
(For Mary and Liam)

If it were up to me
I'd ask Death to wait
for an October Sunday
just after dusk,
the seventh game
of the World Series
an hour away.
I'd make iced tea
the slow way, let it brew
till it was dark
as the inside of an urn,
then I'd pour it
into souvenir mugs
we bought on the boardwalk.
I'd think about the sea,
and the castle we built,
how one of us cried at sunset
when waves taught us
the ache of letting go.
We'd sip tea with lemon
and sugar, share a red bowl
of popcorn and I'd be grateful

for it all: our family's pain
and sweetness, that love survived
these seasons and forgiveness
eased us into second chances.
I'd ask for one last dance,
the three of us close,
the Beach Boys singing
"Warmth of the Sun" and
I'd beg Death
to take me then, before
the music ended,
and let the last touch
of my life be your life
breath upon me,
something to keep
in the shadow of souls
where you'll find me
lonely with God
my arms open,
weeping both your names.

Morning After a Student Dies

My class sits silently long beyond "a moment
of silence" from the P.A. Some weep, most stare
into the quiet for grief has left us only breath
of the heater and the rustle of legs under desks.

When they do speak, it's *Not fair!* over
and over, furious, terrified by cancer at sixteen
and I envy their faith that life's a promise
of goodness, a creed I gave up long ago.

Still, I yearn to be wise, to stun their pain.
But I'm lost in my own darkness. Michael's seat,
solemn as a shrine in the third row, is one more
reminder that the best of love leaves us behind.

I almost utter something like, *Seize life!*
Love while you can! but Becky and Sue grieve
in a trembling embrace and part of me longs
to go to them, press what's left of my heart

to their hearts and, right in front of everyone,
be a living man. I choose instead the safety
of attendance and tally who's here, who's not;
by black lead checks, the scratching of the dead.

STEPHEN DOBYNS

Spider Web

There are stories that unwind themselves as simply
as a ball of string. A man is on a plane between
New York and Denver. He sees his life
as moving along a straight line. Today here,
tomorrow there. The destination is not so
important as the progression itself. During lunch
he talks to the woman seated beside him.
She is from Baltimore, perhaps twenty years older.
It turns out she has had two children killed
by drunk drivers, two incidents fifteen
years apart. At first I wanted to die everyday,
she says, now I only want to die now and then.
Again and again, she tries to make her life
move forward in a straight line but it keeps
curving back to those two deaths, curves back
like a fishhook stuck through her gut. I guess
I'm lucky, she says, I have other children left.
They discuss books, horses; they talk about
different cities but each conversation keeps
returning to the fact of those deaths, as if
each conversation were a fall from a roof
and those two deaths were the ground itself—
a son and daughter, one five, one fourteen.
The plane lands, they separate. The man goes off
to his various meetings, but for several days
whenever he's at dinner or sitting around
in the evening, he says to whomever he is with,

You know, I met the saddest woman on the plane.
But he can't get it right, can't decide whether
she is sad or brave or what, can't describe
how the woman herself fought to keep the subject
straight, keep it from bending back to the fact
of the dead children, and then how she would
collapse and weep, then curse herself and
go at it again. After a week or so, the man
completes his work and returns home. Once more
he gathers up the threads of his life.
It's spring. The man works in his garden,
repairs all that is broken around his house.
He thinks of how a spider makes its web,
how the web is torn by people with brooms,
insects, rapacious birds; how the spider
rebuilds and rebuilds, until the wind
takes the web and breaks it and flicks it
into heaven's blue and innocent immensity.

BRENDAN MOORE

Brendan Moore writes poetry and fiction in the Texas Hill Country, where he lives with his wife and daughter. With twenty-one years of experience as an educator, he teaches English at San Antonio Academy.

Heart Scar

Little daughter,
You lie amidst
the trailing tubes
and beeping screens
of an intensive care unit,
your bed a pale backdrop
to the whiteness of your skin.

Your body is carved soapstone
in blankets: still and silent,
unnatural, like a fish encased in ice,
the pulsating ventilator
by your bed snaking a river
of oxygen to your chest
through a plastic hose
that pulls your soft, little mouth
awry.

Pinioned in a place
beyond consciousness,
paralyzed in vast thoroughfares
of intravenous chemicals,
your eyes gummed with Vaseline,
you still conduct the surging

music of your father's tears
into a majestic symphony of love.

Somewhere in a narrow hour
buried deep in the mellow fuzz of
a hospital night,
I touch your shin
and trace my finger over
the minutest scar,
a tiny, almost invisible curlicue
of whiteness in sun-browned skin,
and I long to see the moment of its creation

a bramble's caress
as you run with T.C.,
your happy shriek as she
snaps playfully at your heels
or a touch of cedar sprig
as your thin, earnest face
hammers at a nail
in your treehouse

or the scrape of a rock
as you ford our creek
in wet weather, your animated words
cascading on me like the rain

or a host of other moments,
imperceptible in their singularity,
unnoticed in the great tide of time.
Yet,
I want to see it more

than anything I have ever
longed for.

Then dawn reaches
through the curtains and
places the pink blush of a kiss
on your cheek
I remove my finger
from your scar, your moment of
unnoticed pain, lost in the
joyful swell of life,
and I know my own scar will
heal.

I bend over and
kiss you, too.

JUDITH M. LAWRENCE

Judith M. Lawrence and Jennifer Nell Lawrence

Judith M. Lawrence, of Vashon Island, Washington, wrote the following in memory of her daughter, Jennifer Nell Lawrence, who died at the age of 10 when she was riding her bicycle and was struck by a motorist.

Jennifer Nell was My Soul, My Hope, My Past, My Future

She *was* me. I had planned on forever and had to watch all our dreams disappear. To let Jennifer go to God, to be his helping guide when he needs her, to reappear as his guiding light, was the hardest thing I'll ever have to endure. I've learned to embrace the challenges of life's changes.

I realized that it was a decision I had to make. Did I want to live or die—to decide—then the fight was on. That was not to say it was easy, but every day, every month, every year was an up-and-down road of tears, sadness, just plain longing to see her bright eyes, hear her quick wit and jokes and laughter.

The journey is long and lasts a lifetime. I thought I would have her company with me longer. Her journey was a wise, short one—she touched each of us deeply with her presence.

My heart was breaking. Can we fix it? Not this time.

To honor her memory I threw red gladiola bulbs all over the garden and planted them wherever they landed. I planted Red Scarlet oak trees for her—red like her cheeks.

I took to looking up at the moon as I was alone after she left, and I missed her face shining up at me with those loving wise brown eyes. I would walk across the grounds at night and it was especially great when the moon was full, with its face shining back at me for comfort. Odd to be so alone and hurting with grief that the moon face felt like comfort.

I used to judge how I was doing with the coming and going of each full moon—second month—then the next year and the 36th full moon—still missing her on and on until ten years had gone by. We get better, we get stronger, we go on. Now when the moonlight appears it lights up my life. I've survived.

I never felt at any time that God had punished me or taken Jennifer. It was simply an accident. I tried to not hang onto her spirit and visualized her as a bird in my hand I needed to let go of, so her spirit could go on and not have to stay here to watch after me.

One day a beautiful small hummingbird was in my greenhouse and as I released it I opened my hand and said, *"Go, goodbye—fly away, Jennifer."*

when Someone dies
their strength is given
to us. It is not taken
away, but it is among us,
with us all the rest of
our lives, untill we too pass
it on

JENNIFER

LOVE

by Jennifer Nell Lawrence

DIANE ROBERTSON

Diane Robertson   Martha "Marti" Nichols

Diane Robertson's daughter, Martha "Marti" Nichols, died at the age of 22 in an automobile accident. After Marti's death, Diane found that phrases relating to her grief experience would come to her, and as they did she wrote them down. Those phrases would finally become the poem, Rise Up Slowly, Angel.

Rise Up Slowly, Angel

Rise up slowly, Angel
I cannot let you go.
Just drift softly 'midst the faces
In sorrow now bent low.
Ease the searing anger
Born in harsh, unyielding truth,
That Death could steal my loved one
From the glowing blush of youth.

Rise up slowly, Angel
Do not leave me here, alone,
Where the warmth of mortal essence
Lies replaced by cold, hard stone.
Speak to me in breezes,
Whispered through the drying leaves,
And caress my brow with raindrops
Filtered by the sheltering trees.
Rise up slowly, Angel
For I cannot hear the song
Which calls you through the shadows
Into the light beyond.
Wrap me in a downy cape
Of sunshine, warm with love,
And kiss a tear-stained mother's face
With moonlight from above.
Then, wait for me at sunset
Beside the lily pond,
And guide me safely homeward
To your world, which lies beyond.
Just spread your arms to take me
In reunion's sweet embrace,
And we shall soar, together,
To a different time and place.

RASHANI

An artist and social activist since childhood, Rashani facilitates retreats and councils throughout the world, holding a space of unconditioned presence, weaving together self inquiry, mindfulness practice, deep ecology, dreambody work, creativity and crazy wisdom. She has designed more than 350 greeting cards, incorporating words from many of her favorite teachers, poets, songwriters, mystics and friends. She has also recorded 14 albums of songs and poems. Rashani is the founder of Earthsong Sanctuary and Kipukamaluhiala'akea on the Big Island of Hawai'i. (www.rashani.com)

When I First Met Death

When I first met death, I was 4 years old. The hummingbirds flew into our windows every spring and summer. Dwarka and I would mix peach juice and water to revive them. When I first met death it was a hummingbird who did not move again. Its tiny body stiffened in my small hand, and I had no idea where its life had suddenly gone. I was speechless for hours. The feathered body where life once pulsed was suddenly motionless. It may have been the first time that no one outside myself could provide me with answers. My 4-year-old mind turned inward, into the inner galaxy of emptiness, and entered the dimly lit pathless path that has carried me for forty-five years since that day.

It was a threshold, meeting death. A portal for my awareness that had not previously considered not existing. I remember after that day lying in bed at night, wondering what there would be if existence had never happened. If nothing existed, what would there be? I lay alone shimmering with a gratitude that still pulses through my being. An utter gratitude for the privilege to exist, to see and hear and smell and taste, and touch and love and move and bring beauty into the world!

When I first met death, I had no idea that it would be the first of many, that I would midwife both of my parents before I turned 40, that I would lose two brothers and a child and my uncle and two aunts and many dear friends. I had no idea that death would be a perennial blooming flower throughout my earthwalk, that its dark talons would grab me again and again and squeeze the life out of me over and over, to render me empty so God could sing through the hollowness of my grief. So poetry and songs, gardens and collages could pour like fragrant light through my being, through the labyrinth of my eyes which have never stopped seeing the Mystery and magic of creation since that long ago day when the hummingbird died in my small brown hand.

There is a Brokenness

There is a brokenness
out of which comes the unbroken,
a shatteredness
out of which blooms the unshatterable.
There is a sorrow
beyond all grief which leads to joy
and a fragility
out of whose depths emerges strength.
There is a hollow space
too vast for words
through which we pass with each loss,
out of whose darkness
we are sanctioned into being.
There is a cry deeper than all sound
whose serrated edges cut the heart
as we break open
to the place inside which is unbreakable
and whole,
while learning to sing.

This poem was written in 1998. My client (and friend) who lives in New Zealand, received a phone call from the Soviet Union saying that her son, Premzia, had been in a serious accident. She took the next plane and arrived a few hours after Premzia died. She had felt shattered for almost a year. I offered to do a session with her and we journeyed to the upper world. She met her radiant son and this song is a true story of what happened. I wrote parts of it also for the baby I lost.—Rashani

A Song for Premzia

You were 17 years old
when your life ended in a car.
You came and went so quickly
from this turning star called Earth.
Who are you truly?
I deeply long to know.

Who were you before your birth
and who are you now?

I journey to discover you
through the tunnel of my heart,
through the corridor of pain,
through the labyrinth of my mind.
I long to find you,
I long to know you.

I journey into dreamtime,
I journey through the dream,
through forgotten fields of childhood,
through sunlit flowing streams.

The veils are growing thinner now,
the veils are turning to cloud,
the veils are vanishing
that separate the worlds!

And there I find you standing:
radiant, glowing Buddha
with a flower in your hand.
Bodhisattva of compassion,
timeless, fearless being,
shadow of an angel.
Your eyes are moonshell oceans
and your face shines like an opal,
your smile is an ancient wingsong,
your heart is a jeweled lotus.

And you came and went so quickly
from this turning star called Earth
and now I find you glowing
as you did before your birth.
Your earthwalk was your chrysalis,
my womb was your cocoon,
now you offer me the flower
blooming in your hand.

My longing turns to ashes,
the tunnel is unfolding,
the corridors are crumbling,
the labyrinth is opening,
as you offer me the flower,
white as night-blooming jasmine.

The gift that you are giving me
is the fragrance of eternity
and the fragrance of eternity
is the sweetest perfume I know,
the greatest gift of all.

This fragrance of eternity
transforms all tears
into dew drops,
transforms all pain into medicine,
transforms all sorrow into song...

Poem to an Unborn Child

Blood pours from my womb.
My spirit a refracted prism.
The surgeon's glance numbs me.

The womb is a tunnel,
a lifetime.

Consciousness sifts through fear.
Fingers grasp my face:
anesthetized hands.
Hollow eye sockets.
Where are my eyes?
Where have they been?

She is torn from my torn placenta:
Shanti Giovanna.
Let me cry, let me bleed
and cry the blood of a century
to lament my unborn child

The flower is a flower
long before it is seen
as a flower.
The interstice of birth and breath
is timeless.

Haiku on Death and Mourning

I.   Where I thought I'd find
       deep anguish, I found instead
       a portal to God.

II.   Death's deep aftermath
       the gloryhole of anguish.
       Suddenly, sweetness.

III.   We mustn't forget:
       the body of the candle
       becomes the pure flame.

IV.   Suddenly laughter
       ripples from the shroud of grief.
       Love's great alchemy.

V.   This breaking open,
       melting again and again.
       But who is breaking?

VI.   Thin interstice
       between breath and the breathless.
       Oh, this fleeting life!

VII.   What once felt like grief
       is the very substance now
       of these open wings.

VIII. Only when my boat
       fully capsized in the waves
       could I see the pearl.

IX.   This precious earthwalk
       quivers like a butterfly.
       The petals of time.

And Like Moonlight
(excerpt from a song)

We can always,
always find our way
to the source
of The Mystery
and like moonlight,
through the night,
into darkness,
through each sadness,
we will shine again.

We are not broken
though the heart
has been so broken open
time and time again.

We are earthlings
born of stardust
and sunlight and motion;
we are shimmering.

From pure essence
we are born
and reborn every moment,
we are awakening.

And like moonlight
through the night
into darkness,

through each sadness,
we will shine again.

Six Months After Your Death
(Written for her mother, Christina Harris, about the scattering of her ashes.)

Here where the rivers meet
Mist gathers colder
Than in a dream

Earth and sky
The song and the cry
Are wed and one
Between
Blurred contours
Of mountain and cloud

The heart's longing
Endowed and deep
Like prisms in the wind
When we scattered your ashes

The moon
A golden hawk bell
In talons of the dawn.

CHRISTINA HARRIS

I want to share a poem that my mother, Christina Harris, wrote after losing her first-born son, Charles, my 19-year-old brother. He died in Spain and we did not make it to his funeral. I was 12 years old.
—Rashani

Some Very Young Escape

Some very young escape
Into a gentler world.
I did not go to him
To say goodbye
To kiss his first soft beard
And brackish hair
To touch his long sweet fingers
That made music into waterfalls.

I did not throw iced stones
Into his winter box
Built specially long
It was his twentieth year.
I could not let him go.
My heart moved over
And I hold him still.
It was he who taught me how to love
When first small fingers
Held me to his breast
And by his dying I learned
To bear the pain
That would come after,

And to read the
Distance between stars.

DEBORAH LINDSAY O'TOOLE

Deborah Lindsay O'Toole believes that if the words she writes touch a well-known or even secret place in someone's heart, she's doing her job. In a quaint old Dallas neighborhood, she shares her garden and her home with family, friends and pets.
To purchase a signed print of any of her verses: (214) 828-0730; thepoem-lady@sbcglobal.net, 5410 McCommas Boulevard, Dallas, TX, 75206

My Loss, Heaven's Gain

I thought of you today—not once,
but oh so many times;
I felt my heart fill up with tears,
and hoped you wouldn't mind.

I struggle with your absence
and wish to see your face,
for now there is a void on earth
that time will not erase.

And yet I hear inside my dreams,
when stars unveil the night,
the angels whispering tenderly
that you are at their side.

And often they remind me
as I go about my day
that all my deepest love for you…
is just a prayer away.

Loved Child

Days of joy, then lonely ones,
loved darling gone away...
while others care and comfort me,
they cannot know I stay
in constant thought of you, dear one
though surely you must hear
prayers I send to heaven and my longing tears.
Cherished child of my delight,
I'll love you deep and ever,
for souls as ours can't be unbound
or by time's drift be severed.
In this life you're not forgot,
sweet darling gone away...
within my dreams, inside my heart
loved angel you will stay.

JENNIFER J. MARTIN

A eulogy written with love in honor and memory of Mike del Rio and for his beautiful family, December 2, 1997:

Angel Heart

Sometimes I called him Mike, but most often I called him Mikey. It was a term of endearment, a name my son called him, a name filled with friendship and deep affection. They were best friends. Perhaps it was the gift of childlike innocence and joy that Mike never lost that made this name best suit him.

On occasion I called him Miguel, which seemed to better suit the expression of the artist he dreamed of becoming and the beautiful combined cultural heritage he received from his family. His physical being was an example of perfection—healthy and beautiful. Deep expressive eyes reflected his tender, sweet soul. His handsome face would defy the blade of a sculptor or an artist's brush on canvas.

Mike was a unique individual—one of a kind. He didn't dress like anyone else. He had his own sense of style complete with jewelry, hats and sandals that captured his mood. He was a free spirit longing to express his artistic soul, a gypsy with a need to take leave of the trappings of the world and paint a colorful picture. When he dressed for an occasion, he didn't make a statement—he *was* a statement.

Mike was at home in nature. He loved spending time at Friedrich Park, a natural game preserve park in San Antonio. When he told me of a sunny Saturday or Sunday afternoon he had spent in Friedrich Park, his eyes sparkled and his face always reflected the peace he found there on long solitary walks among the hiking trails. He would tell his mother that it was his *church,* a place where he found peace.

Mike spent most of his adult life in search of inner peace. He lived his life with a handicap that was not reflected in any physical aspect, which seemed to make it harder for him. It didn't show to the outside world. It is said that when God closes a door, he always leaves a window open. For Mike that window came in the form of his family and friends. He was blessed with the loving support of his mother and father, Colette and Carlos; his brother Carlos W. and his wife, Sherry; and sisters Roxanne and her husband Rod, and Denise and her husband Richard. Each one loved him unconditionally and attempted to provide a safety net within which he could rest and grow strong in the security of their love.

Ultimately, it was not possible for Mike to be like us—and for that I am grateful. For in Mike being who he was, he taught me many things. He taught me about the gift of laughter—a gift for dealing with that which would defeat you—a space in which we could defy aspects of the world that we could not change.

He taught me also of the act of deliberateness. Deliberateness comes in many forms. It comes in the form of Mike walking through my back gate every day and always stopping to pet the cat that welcomed him. He didn't take just a second to pass his hand over the top of the cat's head. But instead, he would crouch down and call her by name, always spending several minutes, rubbing first her head and then waiting patiently until she rolled over on her back. With expectation and great trust, she waited for Mike to rub her tummy the way she liked it.

Deliberateness also comes in the form of perfection. It came in the form of Mike painting a set of French doors of an old Victorian house we restored. Slowly and methodically he colored the doors with their new pumpkin shade in the early afternoon. I, however, was not living in the moment but was more concerned with whether or not they would be dry enough to hang by nightfall.

Finally, my husband said with a smile, "Mikey, they're just doors, they're not going to hang in the Louvre." It is possible to live in the moment and live your life with deliberate perfection. The doors were painted perfectly, and they were dry enough to hang by early evening. Mike lived in the moment, sometimes unable to deal with future plans or tomorrow. But he lived those days with deliberateness, perfection and laughter as his companions.

On November 29, Mike released himself from this world in silence, much as a bird releases a feather from its wing, and our world was forever changed.

In Kahlil Gibran's book *The Prophet*, when he spoke of joy and sorrow, he wrote, "When you are sorrowful look again in your heart, and you shall see that in truth you are weeping for that which has been your delight."

Mikey was my delight, my friend, and my teacher of many things.

A dear friend of mine, Linda Svoboda, selected the following words to be engraved on her son's headstone: "You can't weep for people who have left more in this world than they took out."

My world is a richer and better place because Mike was here.

Yesterday, I spoke with a mutual friend, telling him of Mike's death. He paused for a moment and said, "Mike showed me his soul several times. It was like looking at a star—the splendor of the light shining brightly. But it was a light that you could never capture and hold."

Sometimes, we are privileged to live with great souls. Their time on earth is often brief, yet ever so tender. But in their absence, they leave, as Mike did, enough star dust to help us find our way through the darkness and into the light.

May the angels open wide the gates to paradise for you, Mikey, and may the luminous star that you are always shine brightly in the heavens to help us find our way.

Today, we give you back to God—who has always loved you as much as we do.

Written for my friend, Carmen Compian, and her family on the loss and burial of their daughter, Kathleen Compian Lopez.

A Father's Farewell

Kathleen Compian Lopez died in her sleep on April 4, 1993, at the age of 24. Her mother and my friend, Carmen, called me that Sunday to tell me the news. I cried and felt the pain in my own heart expand. I had lost my only child two years earlier. I knew her pain and also knew what lay ahead of her and her husband, Tony.

I had not known Kathy a long time, but she had a tremendous impact on my life. As a result of a car accident at the age of 19, she was left a quadriplegic and lived within severely restrictive boundaries for five years. She taught me about the true spirit of living and showed me time after time the love she had for life. She was a champion.

On the day that I first visited the funeral home, Kathy's father had placed a large photo album in the foyer with beautiful pictures and mementos of his daughter's life, including her driver's license that spoke to me of a happier time, before the accident, when she easily drove a car or climbed the hills of the outdoors that she so loved. On the page opposite a picture of Kathy in her wheelchair, her father had written, "There are no wheelchairs in heaven." As I reflected on the pages, I knew that Tony was happy his daughter had been set free, but a father's heart was shattered.

In the chapel, only Tony, Kathy's father, and Anthony, her brother, were present. I took a seat in a pew near the front. Kathy's father and brother were selecting some of her favorite tapes from her collection (she was an avid fan of jazz and Tejano music). They had placed a small tape player near the head of her casket. As the music played, in the soft light of the chapel, I observed Anthony, who was leaning over his sister's casket, *talking* to her, asking her questions about how she liked the music. I felt her spirit in the chapel, and I knew her soul was free from the body that once held it captive.

A few moments later, I noticed Tony standing at the head of Kathy's casket. He delicately stroked his daughter's raven black hair, gently brushing back her bangs from her forehead. (I remembered stroking my son's hair just like that when he lay in his casket). The expression on Tony's face and the emptiness in his eyes reflected his pain. Finally, the silent stream of tears down his face told the story of a father's broken heart.

On the day of the funeral, the aisles of the large Catholic church were reserved for Kathy's handicapped friends and their wheelchairs—proud bright symbols of triumph over their challenged lives. They knew, all too well, the emotional frustration Kathy endured and ultimately accepted with absolute grace into her life.

As the Mass began, the priest held the chains of a carved silver incense burner over the white-draped coffin. With a slow deliberate swinging movement of his arm, the incense smoke rose upward toward heaven. I remember how very ancient this ritual must be and how deeply it stirred my feelings.

Following the Mass, we proceeded to the cemetery. Because of Kathy's great love of music, her family had arranged for a mariachi band to play and sing their last songs for her at the gravesite. The mariachis were all Hispanic and wore the typical silver-studded black charro suits, white shirt, black tie and boots. All the songs they sang were in Spanish and, for once, I was grateful I didn't understand them. They say that music is a universal language and by the rhythm and tone of the guitars, violins and trumpets, I knew the songs spoke of loss and of saying goodbye to someone you love. Everyone present who understood the lyrics to the songs wept more than those who did not.

Following the ceremony at the gravesite, Tony stood over his daughter's open grave—her flower-covered casket had already been lowered into the ground. People passed by, hugged him, shook his hand and expressed their condolences. But, over and over again, his gaze returned to Kathy's casket in the ground.

How does a father say goodbye to his princess? The answer is easy: He doesn't. He simply loves her enough to allow her to live in another special kingdom where she can freely walk its garden paths, pick bouquets of flowers and sing her new song.

~

Beloved Bonds of Siblings

~

TARA LEWIS

Tara Lewis was 15 when she had a school assignment to write an analogy about her family. Her little brother, Heath, died at the age of 4½ when he was hit by a car.

The Garden

My father was the seed, brought by the wind, that wasn't there to see the garden grow.

The sun is my brother, who watched over us from above, but didn't live with us.

My mother is the rose, who looks strong and sturdy, but is quite delicate on the inside.

My sister is the dandelion that grows wildly and needs to be tamed and

I am the flower that stands the tallest in the garden, watching as the seasons change.

COURTNEY RABALAIS

The following is a letter from Courtney Rabalais to his brother, Lee, who died at the age of 14 of bone cancer.

Dear Lee

Dear Lee,

I can't believe it has been almost nine years since I last saw you. Every day I awaken, I feel I should be one step closer to moving on, but as more time passes, I know now that moving on is not an option. You will always be with me in each stage of life that I move through, and I wanted to take the time to reflect on my memories of our time together before Meredith and I begin our next stage of life, marriage.

I remember the Elk's club, and the cool water that we used to swim and play in almost each and every day during the hot summers in Louisiana. I remember the long uncut grass of the levee behind our house that we used to take Nikki on walks through. I remember the root of the tree in our front yard that we used to ramp our bikes off of and proceed to ask each other how much air we got. I remember the PB&J's that we used to eat at the dining room table for lunch every day.

I remember the skiing trips we used to take each year and how we always left Mom in the dust at the top of the slopes. I remember the sweet smell of oranges that we would share during halftime of our soccer games. I remember the cold wet days we would spend together with Dad hunting ducks. I remember the bike explorations we used to go on through the neighborhoods of Glenwood Lane. I remember the countless hours we would spend playing basketball in the driveway. I remember the holding pond where we used to go to do things we weren't supposed to, where Mom wouldn't catch us.

I also remember the first time you sat out a soccer game because you said your knee was hurting. I remember finding out that the tumor in your knee was cancer and not knowing what to do or say or what was going to happen to you. I remember the long nights at Shands Hospital where you were receiving chemo.

I remember the day we found out the cancer had disappeared, as well as the day months later that we found out it had resurfaced throughout your body. I remember the talk mom had with me, saying that the probable end result of this reoccurrence would be your death. And, finally, I remember the long walk across that soccer field as Dad approached me, and knowing long before he reached the sideline that you had passed on.

I will never forget the times that we shared together, the good and the bad. I can't imagine my life without these memories and am thankful for every one of them.

There is a special bond between siblings that only siblings can relate to. This bond feels just as strong to me today as when you were still here, and I have no doubt it will continue with me for the rest of my life.

Your bro,
Courtney

~

Letters from Friends and a Gift

~

DEAN KIRKPATRICK

Learning to Fly

I was a 50-year-old flight school student when I met Kelly Hales.

Fulfilling a lifelong dream to become a pilot, I was working full-time and taking flying lessons on weekends. Learning to fly is hard work, and my ground school was made doubly hard by Alyce Taylor, the no-nonsense aviator who owned the flight school. Alyce had trained one of the Apollo astronauts to fly, and she knew what it took to make a pilot.

She had a heart of gold, but Alyce believed that anyone who was licensed by the government to fly an airplane should know *a little something*. That *little something* was an in-depth knowledge of FAA regulations, navigation, weather, radio communications, chart reading and many other things.

Learning to fly is also expensive. In those days, the Cessna 152 I trained in cost $50 for every hour the propeller turned, and my licensed flight instructors cost another $15 per hour.

All this is to say that after two years, when I passed my check-ride, I was tired and broke. And my early romantic notions of joyfully soaring with the birds had been lost to the practical requirements of flying a private plane.

My brand new pilot's license, however, also enabled me to carry passengers, and one of my first was Kelly's mother, Jennifer. Shortly after our flight to Enchanted Rock, I received a thoughtful thank you card that turned my attitude around. It was signed by Jennifer and Kelly. "Fly for us all," Kelly had written on the card.

The encouragement of Kelly's poignant words reminded me of how lucky I was to have the opportunity to be a pilot, and made me realize the importance, in Kelly's eyes, of what I had accomplished.

Kelly's simple message also caused me to recall the joy I experienced when I first began to control an airplane in flight—joy that Kelly recognized, but might never experience for himself without help. Because of his physical challenges, Kelly had little hope of earning a license, or even of taking flying lessons.

This realization gave me an idea. I decided Kelly *should* still get a chance to pilot an aircraft, brief though it might be. Seated beside me in an airborne Cessna, Kelly would take control—he would push the yoke forward and feel the airplane dive, then pull the yoke back and see the nose rise as we climbed. While I pushed the rudder pedals, he would turn the wheel, banking the airplane to the left and then to the right.

We would dive and climb and turn until he had a smile on his face so big that it would live in his heart forever. As he knew the feeling of controlling a machine that rides the wind. I believed he would love it in the way that he had reminded me to love it.

But God had other plans for him, and before we could take off together, Kelly left the confinement of the earth in another way.

I don't usually save cards or letters, but *this card*, that chose me to *Fly for us all,* went in my flight bag, together with a picture of Kelly. The card, the picture, the memory of Kelly flew with me everywhere, and they still inspire me.

JACK BROWN

Kelly, I Remember

Kelly, I remember…

You came to me with eyes so bright—
showed me your own inner light,
and you gave a lesson up to me—
that I've become the person I'd hoped to be.

You stood before me, tall and proud,
said "I am loved," right out loud.
You smiled a smile, big as could be
and shared your love of self with me.

I shone my love of self on you, and
it seems you learned a lesson, too…
that people loved you just as you are
and saw your heart—*a bright shining star.*

JONNIE WRIGHT

Finding Freedom

Too few times our lives are blessed by someone who comes into it. But perhaps that is God's way of causing us to treasure their time with us so dearly.

Kelly was one of those *extra* special people. I will carry him in my mind and heart always. His impish smile, and laugh and twinkling eyes would make my day brighter and happier. Sharing thoughts was his way of saying to loved ones "This is my world and welcome to it." He touched each of us near him with his aura. One time he told me to take life by the tail and shake it when he saw me discouraged and to take one day at a time to enjoy each for its uniqueness.

A child always mirrors his environment and is a product of the love and care, or the lack of it. Kelly bubbled over with the love you gave him, and tried with unrelenting effort to give a share of it to those who came in contact with him.

God blessed us with Kelly, and our memories will hold him close to us forever. We all know he was a complete person inside with an unencumbered spirit. Now he has been freed from his earthly physical impairment and his soul is with the Lord who has always loved him as you have.

All my Love and Prayers,
Jonnie

JOYSA MABEN WINTER

Written in honor of the six-year anniversary of Kelly's death.

Beloved

If I could send a valentine to heaven…
I would use the Internet, because it's
the surest way to navigate the
stars of cyberspace.

If I should send up a valentine,
I would weave a tale of princes
and pyramids—where deserts
yawn into the horizon and where
all desires come true.

If I should send a valentine to heaven
on ancient parchment from the
Song of Songs, I would tell my
angel brother how much I miss
the tango we never got to dance
but how much, so many light years away,
he still warms and dances and
enchants my heart.

You are my beloved, and my beloved is mine

Will you save me the last dance?
I would whisper, on the wings
of a valentine,
…if I could.

CAROLYN RICE

My friend Carolyn Rice, also a bereaved parent and lover of Indian culture, once sent me a card with a silhouette of a white bird in flight, and the words "It's me" printed on the outside. On the inside were the words "Just checking in on you." She included a cut-out angel from white paper, folded in half with a feather tucked inside. Signing it "Love Kelly," here is the poem she wrote:

If Words Were Like Feathers

To Mom—
If words were like feathers
That float on the wind,
I'd send you a message
To help you to mend.
I'd tell you I love you;
You know that I do.
I'd tell you to watch
For the light in the blue,
Our worlds are together.
I'm always close by.
I love when you laugh;
I hear when you sigh.
Live life to the fullest,
And teach others to live.
It's what you taught me.
To love is to give.

Love,
Kelly

The Hopi Indians believe the feather is a sign of hope and a sacred gift. So I am always amazed when I find a feather on days when I am especially missing Kelly. Once, on my birthday, I asked for a sign from Kelly that he was with me that day. Pulling into my mother's driveway, I found a black feather sticking straight up in her front yard.

Kelly loved sending greeting cards to family and friends. On my birthday, it was not uncommon for him to buy me two or three cards to express all he wanted to say. Because I missed his sentiments so much, for several years after his death I asked my husband and mother to continue to pick out a card they thought Kelly might have sent me on my birthday, Christmas, or for Mother's Day, and sign his name. They both did this because they knew how much it meant to me.

Note: I always signed my cards to my husband, family and friends, "Love Always, Jennifer." Kelly must have liked that, as he signed his cards the same way—except for the last card I ever received from him, a Christmas card, which he had signed "*Forever* Love, Kelly." He must have known it would be his last time to tell me his love was forever, and for always.

JENNIFER J. MARTIN AND LINDSAY RUSLER

In 1987, three years prior to Kelly's death, a friend of mine, Lindsay Rusler, who does automatic writing, transcribed this during a writing session we did together. I think the message is profound.

A Gift from the Sky People

The Indian world of tranquility begins with the sign of the bear and the understanding of great oneness. If all of you would take time now to see yourselves as one with rock and fire, water and light. Then we will start again. We will start this part with manna. We will concentrate for meditation time on the water and fire and go on to writing after manna—the base of all that is heavenly.

As the eagle flies through the great gulfs of wind and air, the screaming of his voice is shaking the very stones and rocks below. So the breaths of the wind go down the passages of the heart and bring to you a deep and lasting song you are here to sing. We will pray to manna to bring the song of life and not the song of death to this fireplace. But do not scream down the channels of light. Go slowly and look at each passing rock and cliff as we are flying.

The great cottonwood is bowing to the heat of the blazing sun. Oh great tree, why do you bow? It is for all to bend to the will of the wind. Only then, and with the joy of bending, do we see the sky as a bird and not as a worm. Oh great one, you release a feather from your wing. Why does the feather not fly when the bird can?

We will watch the sun melt the snows from the red cliffs and as the snow melts into streams and runs down the cliff sides, it makes paths so deep the cliff wrinkles its face like an old man. Old cliff and old man, are you one?

We will walk to the edge of the cliff, and I will fly and you will stay. We will always meet together, yet one has wings and one flies not...

◆   ◆   ◆

This transcribed message speaks to my heart of bending to the way of heaven in our grief, of bending like the tree, of yielding all of ourselves to the waves of feelings that come over us.

We would all be served well to acknowledge the message hidden in the words, "and with the *joy* of bending do we see the sky as a bird and not as a worm." My personal experience with this philosophy has been found in my ability to find peace when I focus my attention upward toward the sky and not down to the earth. When I am able to spiritually focus on my loss, I begin to feel less sorry for myself and begin to understand my loss as the beginning of a journey to my soul. In my grief, I questioned why this happened in my life. I questioned existence, death, sorrow, joy, the universe and whether or not I would be able to continue living and why I was still here.

This portion of the message from *The Sky People* is especially close to my heart: "We will walk to the edge of the cliff and I will fly and you will stay—one has wings and one flies not." At the moment of death, Kelly's spirit flew from the edge of the red cliff into the expansiveness of heaven's blue, and I was left standing at the edge of the cliff with tears streaming down my face as the immensity of his death broke me open to the journey of a lifetime—*a journey to my soul.*

JULIE BERGERON

Brance Rueben Bergeron's Footprints

Julie Bergeron is a wife, mother and gifted artist. Her painting I Give My Tears *was, in Julie's words, "Painted to reflect the devastation of losing a child and the process of healing through God's love." The Bergeron's infant son, Brance Rueben, was born on July 24, 1978, and died that same day, living only three hours.*

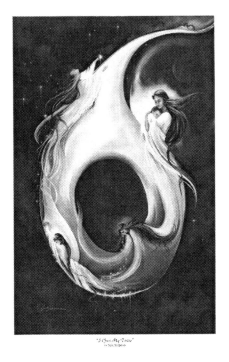

"I Give My Tears"

I Give My Tears

When a child is torn out from human grip as a result of death, our emotions are thrown into despair, depression, emptiness and uncontrollable tears. The pain is still there and will always tug at our emotions.

I learned that if I were to heal, I needed to give my tears to God along with my child, so that God could continue to work in my life and bring his light on each tear that I shed.

> If God's light is on my tear,
> those tears will always shine
> with the beauty of the rainbow.

I Give My Tears prints are available
Large (17" x 25") $30
Small (7½" x 11") $12

Cards
(4 ¼" x 5 ½") Blank Inside $1.30
Phone Order: (719) 687-1815

Soulumination was founded by Seattle photographer Lynette Johnson in response to increasing media attention to, and requests for, her portraits of seriously and terminally ill children. Soulumination's mission is to celebrate the lives of these children by capturing on film the spirit and grace of children who deeply touch their parents' lives but who typically will not live long enough to see their first or second birthday.

Soulumination helps families celebrate the lives of children facing life-threatening illness by donating thoughtful, sensitive, professional portraits of these children and their families. Our mission is informed by personal experience with grief over the loss of children, and by current psychological research that demonstrates the tremendous value pictures can play in helping grieving families recover from the loss of a child.

Our thoughtful, sensitive, donated professional photographs become an important aid to bereaved family members as they work through their life-long grieving and healing.

Finally, Soulumination hopes to use its portraits to put real, human faces on devastating childhood diseases and conditions. Many of these diseases are little more than exotic names (Tay-Sachs, Leigh's syndrome, hydrocephalus, etc.) that are often ignored by our media, and which consequently receive little attention or money for research into their cure or prevention. When appropriate, Soulumination offers portraits to foundations supporting research on a given disease or condition.

Soulumination also provides consulting, educational services and support material to hospitals, hospice groups and photographers who want to create similar photography projects.

Brandon, born March 5, suffers from Leigh's syndrome

Judah, born with severe chromosomal disorder, Trisomy 13
July 22, 2005—November 3, 2005

Soulumination

5201 11th Avenue NW

Seattle WA, 98107

(206) 297-0885

www.soulumination.org

~

Suggested Reading
and Other Resources

~

Recommended Reading

Alex Cord

A Feather In The Rain
"Alex Cord began writing this book as a journal to help him deal with the grief that threatened to engulf him following the death of his son. He says that soon after he started writing, the story began to take on a life of its own. His many Western roles plus a lifetime spent as an accomplished horseman enabled him to provide a gripping reality that will capture and hold the attention of everyone who opens this book."—*Excerpt from the back cover*

Amy Kuebelbeck

Waiting with Gabriel: A Story of Cherishing a Baby's Brief Life, a Story of a Family's Love and a Difficult Choice
"'You have a beautiful baby,' the ultrasound technician said quietly. She was studying the flickering images on her screen, staring intently at the shadows of the tiny heart. I think she had already seen that our baby was going to die."—*Excerpt from the inside cover*

Anne McCracken and Mary Semel

A Broken Heart Still Beats (After Your Child Dies)
"A remarkable collection of poetry, fiction and essays by a journalist and a social worker, both of whom have lost a child. *A Broken Heart Still Beats* gets to the heart of this hardest of truths."—*Excerpt from the back cover*

Antoine de Saint-Exupéry

The Little Prince
"A wise and enchanting fable that, in teaching the secret of what is really important in life, has changed forever the world for its readers...It will capture the hearts of readers of all ages."—*Excerpt from the back cover*

Barbara D. Rosof

The Worst Loss: How Families Heal from the Death of a Child
"Here is a book filled with sensitive empathy and compassionate wisdom. Barbara Rosof is a professional caregiver who genuinely understands the broken heart of the grieving parent. She has completely captured my mind and heart with the depth of her insights. This is an amazingly comforting book for any bereaved parent and a *must* for all professionals."—*Andrea Gambill, editor,* Bereavement *magazine*

Bill Guggenheim and Judy Guggenheim

Hello From Heaven! A New Field of Research—After-Death Communication—Confirms that Life and Love are Eternal
"*Hello From Heaven!* is the first complete study of an exciting new field of research called After-Death Communication or ADC. This is a spiritual experience that occurs when a person is contacted *directly* and *spontaneously* by a family member who has died. During their seven years of research, the authors collected more than 3,300 firsthand accounts of people who believe they have been contacted by a deceased loved one."—*Excerpt from the back cover*

Elisabeth Kübler-Ross, MD

Death: The Final Stage of Growth
"Once we come to terms with death as a part of human development, the author shows, death can provide us with a key to the meaning of human existence."—*Excerpt from the back cover*

Elizabeth Stone

A Boy I Once Knew: What a Teacher Learned from Her Student
Elizabeth Stone is willed the diaries of a former student who has died of AIDS (and whom she hasn't seen in twenty five years) and in reading them begins to reckon with the imminent death of her mother, coming to understand that people die but our relationship with them can evolve and endure. Visit: www.aboyionceknew.com

George Anderson and Andrew Barone

Walking in the Garden of Souls: George Anderson's Advice from the Hereafter, For Living in the Here and Now
"The souls are communicating to us in a way they have never done before. Perhaps it is because they know we are beginning to listen."—*Excerpt from the back cover*

Lessons from the Light: Extraordinary Messages of Comfort and Hope from the Other Side
"For the first time, George Anderson, the world's premiere medium, offers a personal first-hand glimpse of the Other Side, and brings a message of hope and love for all, based on the illuminating lessons of his life's work."—*Excerpt from the back cover*

Harriet Sarnoff Schiff

The Bereaved Parent
"This is the only book of its kind for parents whose child has died—and for all who want to help them."—*Excerpt from the back cover*

Isabel Allende

Paula
"*Paula* is a soul-bearing memoir that seizes the reader like a novel of suspense.
When Isabel's daughter, Paula, became gravely ill and fell into a coma, the author began to write the story of her family for her unconscious child."—*Excerpt from the back cover*

James Van Praagh

Talking To Heaven: A Medium's Message of Life After Death
"As in the case of James Redfield's *The Celestine Prophecy,* once in a while a book comes along that unexpectedly soars to the bestseller lists simply because it feeds a specific spiritual hunger. *Talking to Heaven* is one such book."—*Amazon.com editorial*

Heaven and Earth: Making the Psychic Connection
"Let this book be your guide to developing your natural psychic gifts, to experiencing spirit contact firsthand, and to empowering yourself to live a better life. It is my desire that everyone experience the profound connection between heaven and earth, and that this book help you do so."—*James Van Praagh*

Joel Martin and Patricia Romanowski

We Are Not Forgotten: Messages of Love and Hope from the Other Side
"In this national bestseller, *We Are Not Forgotten*, psychic medium George Anderson began a journey toward the infinite possibilities of life after death. In *We Are Not Forgotten*, he takes us one step closer to the other side."—*Excerpt from the back cover*

We Don't Die: George Anderson's Conversations with the Other Side
"It is one of the most convincing accounts of communication with the deceased."
—*Amazon.com editorial*

Marcus Bach

I, Monty
"*I, Monty* is both the unique story of one butterfly, and the universal story of mankind's unending search for immortality."—*Excerpt from the back cover*

Maria Housden

Hannah's Gift: Lessons from a Life Fully Lived
"Every once in a while a book appears that is so special, it is destined not just to be read but to be cherished, to be passed from one reader to another as a precious gift. Filled with wisdom and grace, *Hannah's Gift* is one such book."—*Excerpt from the back cover*

Mitch Carmody

Letters To My Son: A Journey through Grief
"A very powerfully written book about death, grief, loss and recovery. Authored by a grieving father whose 9-year-old son died following a two-year battle with a recurring malignant brain tumor. During the months that followed his son's death, the author wrote letters and poems to him posthumously as a catharsis for his grief."—*Excerpt from the back cover*

Molly Fumia

A Child At Dawn
"A beautiful, soulfully written narrative about one mother's search for meaning in the death of her child."—*Excerpt from the back cover*

A Piece of My Heart: Through the Grief of Miscarriage, Stillbirth, or Infant Death
"Ultimately denied a safe place to live through their grieving, Molly Fumia provides that safe place where grieving can lead to healing."—*Excerpt from the back cover*

Honor Thy Children: One Family's Journey to Wholeness
"This heartbreaking story of a Japanese/American couple who experienced the tragic deaths of all three of their children, two from AIDS, one a murder victim—records the family's trajectory from homophobia and denial to emotional healing."—*From Publisher's Weekly*

Safe Passage, Words to Help the Grieving
"With *Safe Passage*, Molly Fumia offers a compassionate, understanding companion for the difficult yet transformative journey from the grief and heartache of loss to the hope and possibility of love eternal."—*Excerpt from the back cover*

Nicolas Wolterstorff

Lament for a Son
"Wolterstorff, a well-known Christian philosopher, lost his 25-year-old son to a mountain climbing accident. His reflections in the wake of the tragedy are at times deeply personal, but always he expresses a prayerful anguish with which most bereaved parents will identify."—*Library Journal*

Paula D'Arcy

Gift of the Red Bird: A Spiritual Encounter
"*Gift of the Red Bird* is a deeply moving account of a spiritual journey where darkness and light, sorrow and love, resistance and freedom became integrated—and a soul (Paula's) is able to soar again like a bird set free. You will soar too."—*Macrina Wiederkehr*

Song For Sarah: A Young Mother's Journey Through Grief and Beyond
The author describes her book: "These letters for my daughter, Sarah, are part of the actual journal I began in 1973 when I first learned I was pregnant. I little guessed then that they would be my detailed recollection of a time and a life that was suddenly and unkindly ended. And yet the pain and outrage of death eventually brought me such insight and growth that these words for Sarah truly became not a cry but a song."—*Excerpt from the back cover*

Raymond Moody, MD

Reunions: Visionary Encounters with Departed Loved Ones
"*Reunions* is the ground-breaking study of making contact with apparitions of the dead."—*Excerpt from the back cover*

Shelly Wagner

The Andrew Poems
"In 1984, Shelly Wagner lost her young son, Andrew, in a drowning accident. The poetry contained in the pages of this book is some of the most

stunningly eloquent and beautifully written I have ever read. I highly rec-
ommend this book to everyone."—*Jennifer J. Martin*

Stephen Levine

Who Dies? An Investigation of Conscious Living and Conscious Dying
"While many books have dealt with the 'stages of death,' and particularly
the stages of acceptance of death, this is the first to demonstrate how to
open to the immensity of living with death."—Excerpt from the back cover

*Meetings at the Edge: Dialogues with the Grieving and the Dying, the Healing
and the Healed*
"With consummate skill, Stephen invites us into the intimacy and subtlety
of living one's dying. Through others' resistance we meet our own;
through others' breakthroughs we greet our own. These extraordinary dialogues take our appreciation of the dying process a giant step forward."—*Ram Dass*

Recommended Music:

CD: *Gypsy Train*

"Wounded Healer"
by singer-songwriter Cary Cooper

*Cary Cooper is a performing songwriter, a mother of two beautiful daughters,
and a wounded healer. She lives near Dallas, Texas, with her partner in music
and life, Tom Prasada-Rao. You may contact her at www.carycooper.com*

CD: *Outside Eden*

"Go To The Water"
by singer-songwriter Kat Eggleston

*Kat Eggleston is a songwriter and singer with several CDs to her credit. She
travels internationally, solo or with other musicians. You may contact her at
www.kateggleston.com*

CDs by singer songwriter Jana Stanfield:

CD: *Brave Faith*
"If I Were Brave"
"Bitter or Better"
"Brave Faith"
"Doesn't Mean that I'm Not Strong"

CD: *Enjoy the Ride and I'm Not Lost I Am Exploring*
"Butterfly"

CD: *Stop, Look and Listen and Playing Favorites*
Angels Among Us

CD: *For My Broken Heart*

"If I Had Only Known"
by Reba McEntire
written by Jana Stanfield and Craig Morris

Who is Jana Stanfield? You've heard her music on 20/20, Entertainment Tonight, Oprah, *the movie* 8 Seconds, *and radio stations nationwide. Her compositions are sung by Reba McEntire, Andy Williams and others; Jana has shared the stages with such performers as Kenny Loggins and the The Dixie Chicks.* www.JanaStanfield.com

Magazines:

Living with Loss magazine
Hope & Healing for the Body, Mind and Spirit (formerly *Bereavement* magazine)
www.livingwithloss.com

Grief Digest magazine
www.griefdigest.com

We Need Not Walk Alone
www.compassionatefriends.org

Other healing resources:

www.centering.org
www.i-remember.org
www.fireinmyheart.com
www.griefsources.com
www.goodgriefresources.com
www.compassionatefriends.org

Psychic mediums:

George Anderson
www.georgeanderson.com

Voices from Heaven—The Robert Baca Story
www.voicesfromheaven.com

James Van Praag
www.vanpraag.com

REFERENCES

The author has been granted permission to print all materials, including song lyrics, essays and poems, which appear in this book.

A. Powell Davies, *Great Occasions: Readings for the Celebration of Birth, Coming of Age, Marriage and Death,* reprinted with permission Beacon Press

Alice Hoffman, *Advice From My Grandmother,* From: *Family: American Writers Remember Their Own* by Sharon Sloan Fiffer and Steve Fiffer © 1996 by Sharon Sloan Fiffer and Steve Fiffer. Reprinted with permission Pantheon Books, a division of Random House Inc.

Antoine de Saint-Exupéry, *The Little Prince,* © 1943 by Harcourt Inc. Renewed 1971 by Consuelo de Saint-Exupéry English translation © 2000 by Richard Howard, reprinted by permission Harcourt Inc.

Elisabeth Kübler-Ross, *Death, The Final Stage of Growth,* reprinted with permission Simon and Schuster Inc.

Hermann Hesse, *Demian,* © 1925 by S. Fischer Verlag. English language translation © 1965 by Harper and Row Publishers Inc. Copyright renewed 1993. Reprinted by permission of HarperCollins Publishers

Jerome Rothenberg, *Shaking the Pumpkin: Traditional Poetry of the Indian North Americas.* (English version by Anselm Hollo) Reprinted with permission of University of New Mexico Press

Kahlil Gibran, *The Prophet,* © 1923 by Kahlil Gibran and renewed 1951 by Administrators C.T.A. of Kahlil Gibran Estate and Mary G. Gibran. Reprinted by permission Alfred A. Knopf, a division of Random House Inc.

Molly Fumia, *Safe Passage, Words to Help the Grieving,* reprinted with permission Conari Press, imprint of Red Wheel/Weiser

Richard Bach, *Illusions, The Adventures of a Reluctant Messiah.* Reprinted with permission Random House Inc.

Richard Bach, *Jonathan Livingston Seagull.* Reprinted with the permission of Scribner, an imprint of Simon & Schuster Adult Publishing Group,

About the Author

Jennifer J. Martin is an artist and author who lives in San Antonio, Texas, with her husband, John. She has led support groups for bereaved parents and speaks at local nonprofits on coping with the loss of a child and healing after loss.

Jennifer is currently finishing her first novel, *Heaven's Stone*, which tells the story of a woman and a Mayan shaman, who, with the aid of an ancient artifact, penetrates the veil between heaven and earth to allow the grieving mother to see her child one more time. You may reach Jennifer by e-mail at Jennifer@JJMartinStudio.com.

978-0-595-40216-8
0-595-40216-X

Printed in the United States
70225LV00006B/123